"After working with Libby on a number development sites she has proved that her know. education and experience are the reason she has succeeded in the property development sector for so long.

'Millions & Billions in Property Development' is a fantastic step by step guide allowing the reader to absorb 15 years of Libby's knowledge from sourcing the site, site selection, dealing with councils, contractors, architects and agents. Her clear & concise point of view, help guide the reader through the many obstacles of property development, resulting in a comprehensive understanding of how to put a site together and start you on the way to becoming a successful property developer!"

Amanda Gould – Director HighSpec Properties

"If you are looking for a mentor to take your property investing to the next level or to grow your property development skills, this book is for you.

Simple and easy to understand language ensures property development is a skill anyone can learn and implement.

Whether you are looking to make millions & billions in property development or simply build a nest egg through property, this is the fast track to your success.

Definitely a must have for the property buff's bookshelf!"

Fiona Jones – Best-selling author of The Millionaire Books.
Founder of the Millionaire Books & the Millionaire School.

"What an interesting and inspiring read - loved it! We've been wanting to move beyond our current investment strategy and give developing a go and this book has answered so many questions we had on things that seemed so complicated that now we understand. Really easy to digest and Libby is such a realist. Highly recommend!"

Victoria Skik - Investor and Founder Liberty Blue Swimwear

"This book is a real find! Libby writes in everyday language and makes a challenging and complicated subject easy to understand. Her energy comes through the book and is very inspiring!"

Amanda Abbot – Business Consultant

"I have known Libby for 14 years and she has always been a dynamic go getter, action oriented person. Whatever she sets out to accomplished she attains. She has a huge passion for property development which makes her someone to follow and learn from. The multi-million dollar ideas contained in this book are worth 1000 times the price of the book. Read her book and have access to your own personal property development mentor at your fingertips!"

Toney Fitzgerald – Innovator, Entrepreneur, Speaker and Author of *Start Me Up and Don't Bitch Just Get Rich*.

"I have had the pleasure of knowing and working with Libby for many years now. I consider her to be a friend, business partner and possibly most importantly a mentor and coach for me when looking at any development opportunity that presents itself.

Libby and her extensive background in really understanding the complete property development process, has for me, meant that when I have referred a client to her and the team - I know they will not only be supported throughout the whole process of putting a development together, but also that Libby's attention to detail, that she demands of herself will result in my client also achieving all the desired outcomes the project suggested.

Libby, unlike so many other developers in this area has actually undertaken each and every step of completing a development many times for both small and larger developments – Libby has learnt from practical experiences.

Libby's ability to get in and work with her client's one on one, is, I feel one of her most valuable skills, she is personable, friendly, empathetic of one's challenges and supportive - while being there to also lift one's game as a coach.

I highly recommend Libby and her coaching if you're serious about getting real results from your first experiences in developing property."

Duncan Yelds – Mentor Coach & Property Strategist
Co-author of *Millionaire Mentors*

"Libby Lombardo has helped me twice now to obtain development properties.

Her assistance and expertise is greatly appreciated.

When Libby decides she is going to help, she gets going - you can feel the support and total encouragement all the way.

I regard Libby as a friend. She is one to deliver great results, and one of her features is her approachability. I would recommend Libby's services highly."

Henry Blumenthal BA, LLB

"We have known Libby Lombardo from Leverage Property for over 5 years now. She is a true professional who shares her knowledge freely on her successful property developing strategies. We have attended a number of her meetings and workshops where people get the best information and content so that they too can create wealth through property development and property investing."

Jan and Don Milne – CEO Property Achievers Group

"Libby has acted for me as a consultant on two of my projects and I wouldn't work with anyone else. Her extensive knowledge and creativity in the property development space has provided me with an opportunity to both learn and profit in real estate. I consider Libby a good friend and mentor and I look forward to working with her on more deals in the future."

Matthew Stubbs – Managing Director of Stubbs Holdings Pty Ltd

MILLIONS AND BILLIONS IN

PROPERTY DEVELOPMENT

MILLIONS AND BILLIONS IN

PROPERTY DEVELOPMENT

How You Can Make More than Your
Annual Salary in Just One Deal!

LIBBY LOMBARDO

First Edition 2015

Copyright © 2015 Libby Lombardo

National Library of Australia Cataloguing-in-Publication entry:

Creator: Lombardo, Libby.

Millions and Billions in Property Development / Libby Lombardo.

1st ed.
ISBN: 9780994184702 (paperback)

Real estate investment – Australia.
Real estate business – Australia.
Real estate development – Australia.

332.63240994

Published by Author Express
www.AuthorExpress.com
publish@authorexpress.com
1300 887 887

DEDICATION

This book is dedicated to all the people who have the property passion, and strive to do well in life no matter what that is, I really hope this book ignites your property flame!

To my dad who always inspired my love for property and his priceless lessons.

To mum for your endless love.

My husband and beautiful daughter Isabella, my everything and the reasons why, every day!

To Paula for coming into my life and changing it forever, through all the laughs, tears, and triumphs!

Bonus Gift

Simply by purchasing a copy of this book you will have access to a free webinar training program by Libby Lombardo.

Simply go to
www.LibbyLombardo.com/BONUS

TABLE OF CONTENTS

The Libby Lombardo story   1

Chapter 1   The right mentality   7

Chapter 2   Which kind of site do I develop?   17

Chapter 3   Finding your own site   33

Chapter 4   Choosing your site   61

Chapter 5   The F word – Feasibility   77

Chapter 6   DA Day – Getting Development Approval   99

Chapter 7   Getting started with little or no money   111

Chapter 8   Show me the money – financing your deal   137

Chapter 9   The Buy and Negotiations   151

Libby's Last Word   175

About Libby Lombardo   177

Libby's Recommendations   179

THE LIBBY LOMBARDO STORY

I see my story as more 'rags to happiness' than the cliché, rags to riches. It took me now seventeen years of putting one foot in front of the other to get my 'overnight success' - putting the deals together, accumulating experience and expanding my property network. I am living proof that it's not where you start that matters; it's where you end up.

I was born in 1977, far from Sydney's café latte set in the city's western suburbs, the youngest of five children. I felt challenged by education and big classes, and at some point just shut down rather than wound my pride by asking for help. I got expelled in year 7 after long struggles with traditional learning, bouncing between five different high schools. Some teachers tried to stick by me, others gave up, sighing, "You will never amount to anything!" But deep down, I knew different…

The further I fell behind, the more I rebelled against the rules: the only way to keep control that I knew. The other students found me crazy and fun to be around because I was fearless - I mean no fear. I found my niche as a smartarse, and got very good at being bad.

To illustrate my own humble beginnings, I had no money to my name when I embarked upon the property path for the first time! I was a young 19-year-old girl from the burbs, full of ambition, but after my career as a high school rebel I was not keen to join 'the system.' I did not apply myself to scholastic pursuits as a teenager, so I knew a uni degree or conventional 'tick-tock' office job was not my way forward. With the classic early mindset of an entrepreneur, I was looking for a way to really spread my wings. I knew that I was going nowhere fast, and wanted something bigger and better. I was shopping around for a vision, or purpose.

To add fuel to my fire, my Dad - also a born entrepreneur - had lost all his money, business and properties when I was about 12 years of age. Our house and life as we knew it had literally vanished overnight, which only intensified my ambition to get it all back and not only improve their lives, but make up for my own shame at being 'the poor one' at school.

Determined to leave the burbs behind, I knew the first step was to get to Sydney. Moving to inner city suburb, Paddington exposed me to a whole new world of cosmopolitan sophistication: trendy restaurants and wine bars full of well-travelled, fashionably dressed people having smart conversations. I was just starting to soak it all up when fate intervened and I saw an ad in the newspaper seeking a nanny.

It was only a few weeks after getting the position that I realised the enormity of what had happened. I began caring for Paula, the then infant daughter of billionaire, Richard Pratt, who made his global fortune recycling paper and cardboard. On our first trip to New York, already a mind-blowing opportunity for someone who had never left the country, I was soon set straight by Paula's mother: we would be flying on Richard's own personal plane.

So there I stood, a 20-year old with stars in her eyes, ready to board a gleaming $50 million dollar jet, being greeted by an immaculately dressed, rugged man in a black suite with a roguish expression who introduced himself, "Hi, I am RP - nice to meet you." That would be Australia's second richest man, worth in excess of $5 billion dollars. I repeat, $5 billion dollars.

As I sat in the beautifully appointed plane, sinking back into the plush leather, looking out at the infinite starry sky, I realised that this was a high-octane version of the life experience that I had been longing for. Over the years, I travelled the world in the Pratt intimate family circle, continually blown away by their rarefied lifestyle. But it wasn't just the toys that impressed me;

it was Richard Pratt's abilities and mindset. This man embodied persistence, vision, determination and the pursuit of a great deal - something that excited him through his entire journey as an empire builder.

I got my first glimpse of someone who lived his dreams, and thought beyond the wage to the glittering rewards of investment at the end of the rainbow. I had an epiphany: this was the way that I wanted to live. It was Richard Pratt's copy of Robert T. Kiyosaki's *Rich Dad, Poor Dad* that started me on my life as an autodidact (more of that later), teaching myself about wealth and how it works. From the beginning, I knew that this was not about the champagne lifestyle and caviar dreams: I wanted to learn as much as I could from 'RP' and his friends.

By following the advice of the wealthy people in my surroundings, and steeping myself in wealth creation self-help books, I actually achieved my dream of making over $1million in property by the time I was 25 (you'll find more details in following chapters).

But all big journeys in life come with stumbling blocks - and that's where the real lessons begin. My mistake: I thought my dream run would last forever. With that in mind, I got the fancy car that I thought I deserved after all that scrimping, saving and hard work. I focused on the outer signs of success and the next great deal, fired up with all the arrogance of presumption, rather than a contingency plan that would tide me over if the market ever turned. And it did.

When the property bubble burst and developers were not interested in buying my sites and my development applications, I had no cash reserves to draw on, but lots of debt obligations. In other words, I was totally exposed!

This brontosaurus sized life lesson really shook me up. I had no other income coming in, no other way to make the hundreds of thousands required to keep up with my properties and overheads, so I borrowed even more against them. You don't need to be Stephen Hawkins to realise that this finite amount would soon run out, especially as values kept dropping. I couldn't sleep, I couldn't eat and stress was taking its toll on my health. My ego, driving me to prove myself to others, had sent me hurtling on a rollercoaster – headed straight down.

I sold properties at a loss; the car got towed because the lease payments were untenable; the mail got too depressing to even look at anymore. Those are days that you never forget. It took two solid years for the 20/20 hindsight to emerge. Now I cherish the main lesson. Instead of investing my profits on good, solid real estate that paid for itself - which would let me weather any crisis - I had gambled it on speculative deals on the assumption that the money would keep rolling in.

So now I know! Plan for the dark storm when life is all bright and sunny, because it cannot be bright and sunny all the time. I never looked out for the storm clouds, but ask anyone who has been around and they'll tell you - about every 10 years in the cycle, they are just around the corner. So buy yourself a raincoat and always plan for financial stress.

Money can pass through people's hands pretty quickly, but I now know the number one rule of finance: it's not how much money you make, it's how much money you keep that counts.

My path includes having nothing, becoming a millionaire, hitting rock bottom then getting it all back - and more.

I have cautioned you to protect your fortune, now comes the fun part. Let's go make it!

CHAPTER ONE:
The Right Mentality

" If money is smarter than you, you will work for it all of your life. To become the master of money instead, you must be smarter than it. "

CHAPTER ONE: THE RIGHT MENTALITY

Before we get started on the nuts and bolts of how to put together a lucrative development deal, there is a certain mindset that good developers have - and novice developers don't have - that underpins all the techniques and knowledge you are about to learn. You will rise above the pitfalls, and tap into the profits just waiting out there, if you approach each step of the process with the right mentality and never waver.

I know that anyone who is picking up a book about property development is probably pretty savvy about money already, but certain financial philosophies are so core to property development that they bear repeating.

So let's lower the lights, set the mood and adjust your mindset to get you on your way...

DON'T BE AN EMOTIONAL BUYER

It is easy to get passionate and excited about a site that has "potential" written all over it. But you can't fall in love with any property - you have to be in love with the deal. Do the numbers crunch? Will you achieve good sales? Is it risky? What is the council like to deal with? When you go into negotiations, you have to be leading with logic, not emotion.

Time and time again my students have rushed to me with a deal that just excites and engages them emotionally, for whatever reason: pride that they have done the legwork and found a site all on their own; nostalgia that it is in their childhood neighbourhood; the thrill of finding something too good to be true (hint: it usually is); falling in love with the leafy, beautiful street or great north facing light.

By the way, real life developers do this all the time too. And it can even be negative emotion that weds them to a deal: simple arrogance that they can turn a site around when no-one else could; a competitive streak that blinds them to the facts; denial about their ability to raise their finance or service the holding costs.

Whatever the reason, whenever emotion reigns, people will move heaven and earth to make that particular deal work. But they have it the wrong way around.

There is always another deal.

So a good developer ditches the deal that doesn't add up to an acceptable level of profit and moves heaven and earth to find one that does.

The more properties you see, the less you 'fall in love' and the more you keep your cool - and your options open. Once you have tasted a deal that really works from the get go, you'll learn to never compromise. You can always walk away and find another deal; that's the magic and power of not being emotionally attached.

This same detachment will serve you well all throughout the process, from dealing with personalities in the construction company to the fit-out of your finished apartments at the other end. That's when it's crucial to remember that this isn't about building a place that you would like to live in, but about pleasing your BUYER, and building what is feasible for the location, who will snap up your apartment at a high price because they just have to have it.

Remember, you want to SELL to emotional buyers, but you can never be one yourself.
So put your emotions aside, learn the system and play it right.

KNOW THY MARKET

You CANNOT know a good deal when you see it if you don't know the market by heart - so put in the research. You need to pounce on a great deal with confidence, not a gamblers streak or 'gut instinct' alone.

Remember your not buying a typical long term 'investment property' your embarking on a development deal it's a whole different ball game and change of attitude, you have to make the money when you buy the deal.

This is where your passion will come in. Developers who live, eat and breathe an area are the industry leaders, because they have the insider knowledge and connections to stay ahead. They know their sales predictions and forecasts; they gauge community feeling and local gossip; they have a rapport with the agents who give them a first look; they can pounce on a good price or laugh at an inflated one because they know pretty much down to the dollar what the real market value is. They know who will be selling and why - sometimes before the market. Understand the council and the politics.

Whether you stick to the coastal suburbs, only buy in new, up and coming areas, go for light industrial or opt for blue ribbon is only part of the equation. You must develop expertise - in whatever area. Have dinner there, drive the streets, make buddies and steep yourself in real, local knowledge: get a feel for it. This is how I started in suburban Northmead in Sydney's West. I concentrated on one location for so many deals because I knew the area - from the council to the values of each street and everyone that was building buying and selling – I knew it like the back of my hand.

I can show you how to analyse the facts and figures of a locale, but you'll add a real sense of context with hand shaking and on-the-spot experience.

This is an area I studied in Sydney's Little Bay, I knew all about the location, future growth, demographics, council's future plans and requirements, growth and most importantly possible new zonings.

INVEST IN A FINANCIAL EDUCATION

If money is smarter than you, you will work for it all of your life. To become the master of money instead, you must be smarter than it.

There is financial wisdom out there worth its weight in gold. As I touched on in my brief story, my first life-changing book was *Rich Dad, Poor Dad* by Robert T. Kiyosaki. The revelation that a pay cheque was a short-term solution, and that true wealth only comes from investing changed my life. I was totally sold on the concept that money could go out and work for me right away, that I could build wealth through buying, managing, and selling property.

When I read Kiyosaki's central philosophy, rich people don't get rich from their education, they get rich from their 'financial education,' it immediately resonated with me. I studied this book from cover to cover until it became part of my every day thinking process. Then I devoured every one of the books on Kiyosaki's recommended reading list. Sure I was young and naïve, but driven enough to know that those older and wiser were there to teach me, so I took myself to wealth-building university; I constantly listened to self-improvement CDs when driving.

And I'll be an autodidact for the rest of my life as there is always something else to learn.

Rich Dad, Poor Dad reads, "If you are going to build the Empire State Building, you need to build a big foundation." That foundation is your financial education.

Looking back, I realize that even when I stumbled, it was continuing my education, learning about my trade and tapping into the positive reinforcement of personal development that made me successful again - and will keep me winning for the rest of my life.

It is not enough just to make the money. It is absolutely imperative that you learn how to keep the money.

So keep bettering yourself and always believe in yourself. That foundation is what will keep you going when times are tough, the economy is weak, you are out of a job or you're low on cash.

This need to better yourself through self-education is the reason why I developed the 'Leverage Academy Education Program'.

Knowledge is your biggest asset!

Students 'get real' on site and learn!

"The most expensive piece of real estate is the six inches between your right and left ear. It's what you create in that area that determines your wealth. We are only really limited by our mind." - Dolf de Roos

So keep bettering yourself and always believe in yourself.

CHAPTER TWO:
Which Kind of Site Do I Develop?

" *My philosophy is that if you have done all your homework on a property or site, you must make your profit when you buy it.* "

CHAPTER TWO: WHICH KIND OF SITE DO I DEVELOP?

In very simple terms, 'property development' means taking a piece of land and actively doing something to increase the value of it.

The best thing about land is that they are not making any more of it. Find out what is most valuable now, and it will be even more valuable to the buyer!

My philosophy is that if you have done all your homework on a property or site, you must make your profit when you *buy* it. But you will need to go through a series of planned-out steps to *develop* and *extract* that profit.

WHAT ARE MY OPTIONS? WHAT'S ON THE MENU?

There are several different ways to develop properties and make them much more valuable to the next buyer – who will not only pay off your original investment but also make you a profit.

- **Rural Sites:** Buying up raw acreage and upgrading it to the potential residential stage by adding infrastructure such as electricity, water, 'pegging out' boundaries, etc.

- **Land Subdivisions:** Slicing up a large property and selling off the extra land, with or without buildings on it.

- **Land Banking:** Holding onto land for a long time, then reselling it when there is a spike in future capital gain. The land usually makes an artificially high leap in value due to re-zoning, which allows for more development or some added value in the area like a new supermarket.

- **Warehouse Conversions:** Turning light industrial property into residential housing that is highly prized for its wider open spaces, higher ceilings and newly fashionable inner-city, non-suburban history.

- **Unit Block Makeovers and Strata Titling:** Transforming an existing unit block. This can be done from a purely legal standpoint by converting the building from a 'company title' entity, where owners own shares in a board-run corporation, to a more common 'strata title' collection of individually owned and run apartments. Or it can involve a physical rejuvenation and update to add value: landscaping, rendering the brick exterior, building on the rooftop airspace, etc.

- **Unit Development:** Constructing a block of units from scratch, either on an undeveloped block of land or one with an existing property that will need to be demolished. Unit development can range from small blocks of four units to giant complexes with hundreds of separate units and public facilities, including pools.

- **Townhouse Development:** Constructing a block of terraced, usually two-storey houses that share a wall. These are commonly built in smaller numbers of four to six.

- **Commercial/Industrial/Retail:** Constructing non-residential buildings with the needs of manufacturers and businesses in mind, e.g., with glass shop fronts for merchandise display and office space.

These are all perfectly legitimate and potentially profitable areas of property development. If I could clone myself, I'd do them all! But rather than dabble across the board and be a Jack-of-all-trades, I recommend developing mastery in just one small corner of property development. Think big, certainly, but in that one area. You have to ask yourself what kind of property developer you want to be. Come up with a formula that works for you.

I created a formula, and I perfected it through a lot of trial and error over time. When you do this, you get to know what works and what doesn't; you develop strengths and weaknesses; you learn from your mistakes and build up the relevant contacts in your corner of the industry.

Everything from your circle of business friends to knowledge of the relevant council rules for a certain area of property development will keep enriching your next project in the same area.

Because my own personal experience of making real profits lies in the following areas, and because the main focus here is on property development, I will be focusing in this book on the types of sites I have purchased, developed and sold.

There are so many creative ways to make money and structure deals in property development-always be thinking outside of the box.

"Get creative, think outside the box, you make the rules! This is what I love about property development."

RAW AND DA-APPROVED SITES

Raw Development Sites

A raw development site is land that has not been developed yet. It either has a single dwelling or no building at all, and there has been no development application to council regarding the land. Its potential has not been realised yet – thus it is in the 'raw'.

Developing this site involves deciding what is the best use for it, within the parameters of what is permissible in that zone. Then you begin the process of the Development Application ('DA'), whereby you apply to council for permission to build something of greater value on the land – e.g., townhouses where a house now stands, or a small or large block of units. Real estate sales agents often include these bright ideas in advertising, with the proviso STCA, or 'subject to council approval'.

Once you have followed all the steps of the Development Application process and it is granted, your site graduates to the status of 'DA-approved'. This generally makes it more valuable because you can then on-sell the property to a developer who wants to skip the DA process and get straight into building. That developer can then build according to your plans, with full council approval, once they obtain the relevant building applications.

Or you can keep the newly approved site and build on it yourself.

A DA lasts five years before it lapses, but can sometimes be renewed through a new application.

Below you can see pictured one of my door-knocking rezoning projects. A raw development site in Merrylands, Sydney optioned up two houses and we did a DA for 27 units. We teach this exact step-by-step process in our Leverage Academy Education Program. It's a great way to maximise profits and make a lot more money than your average income in just one deal!

The information is obtained from various sources and cannot be guaranteed. You must make your own enquiries as to its accuracy.

The development site

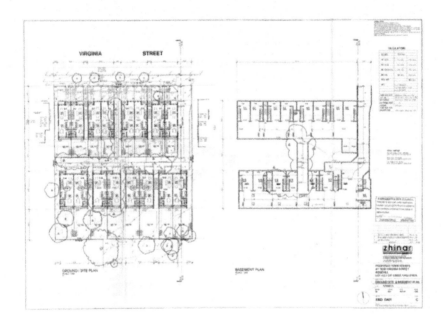

DA plans

Built project

Raw Sites Are Good for Beginners

Taking on a site with no development application is a great way to add value when you are starting out – you can build on the momentum of established players long before you are ready to take on the actual construction yourself.

There are always bigger developers who are too busy on other massive, multi-million-dollar projects to invest their time or block their cash flow waiting for DAs to come through. But they are more than happy to pay you extra for putting the package together when the

DA is done, because they will still make their profit from the construction and can start right away, reducing the holding costs of all their borrowed money.

Developers that have their own building companies like to buy DA-approved sites because they don't have to wait for the DA to be approved while the builders are left idle with nothing to build.

In my early years, before I had the experience to construct new property myself, I would do all the legwork at council, adding value by getting DA approval and then selling the property straight on to someone who had the experience and budget to build, but not the time to get the DA themselves.

Little to No Money Down

There are multiple ways to put little or no money down to control land at this raw stage and make big profits. I talk about this later in Chapter Seven when I discuss options. This is always a big topic at our Leverage Academy events as there is a lot to understand to get it right, but once you learn, you hold the big leverage power!

In a nutshell, what this means is that you can be the pilot fish who sets everything up for the whale.

DA-Approved Sites

A DA-approved site is land that already has an attached development application approved by council regarding improvements that can add value. Taking on a DA-approved site is playing with the big boys in construction. With a raw site, an investor creates something from nothing, taking land and *in theory* making it worth more. But buying land that already has this stamp of approval from the council allows the developer the ability to create *literal* value from the ground up in bricks and mortar – and property sales.

The developer who buys a DA-approved site is free to proceed with construction, subject to subsequent building applications and construction certificate approval for extensions, apartments, townhouses, duplexes, residential developments, mixed-use developments or commercial developments. These properties are then the developer's to rent out, sell off individually or a mix of both.

DA-approved sites are very valuable in the industry because the buyer saves all the time that would otherwise be required for the council's administrative process, and also has certainty because the DA is in the bag. Usually, the bigger the developer, the more they exclusively deal with DA-approved property, to streamline their process.

"Train yourself to see the opportunity, you will never look at things the same again."

RAW SITES – MY FIRST PROJECT

I started in the game with a raw site. I must have had the property development bug from the very beginning, because my very first purchase was also my very first project. No single-girl clichés of a residential unit, 25-year mortgage and wage slavery for me, thanks!

After reading up a storm about property investment, then doing the legwork and approaching local homeowners in the area I was interested in (see Chapter Three on finding a site), I found a seller and bought a home on a 600-square-metre block.

I was very young, but I was happy and proud to have achieved my first goal of starting in the property game. *But I wasn't going to sit around and wait for capital gain – I wanted to add value right away.* I had done my research at council, and I knew that the zoning for this particular street allowed two-storey townhouses – the best way to maximise the return on my investment. I got even more ambitious when the local council explained that if I bought the houses next door to the current site, I could build even more townhouses.

Even though I had no money to construct a whole bunch of townhouses, I had cultivated relationships with many developers and *knew people who did have the money*. After gaining temporary control of the neighbouring houses without having to pay in advance (see Chapter Six), I completed a development application on the property, then sold it on to a more established developer after development approval, for a whopping profit without having to touch a single brick.

I paid $4,300 in option fees to 'hold' the property.

It cost $22,000 to do the DA.

I sold the package at the end of a 14-month period and made a profit of $170,000 (before tax).

I put the theory of what I had learned into practice, and made more money than I had ever seen before with just one deal – a year's executive salary!

Concept Image

Sometimes I am the one to take a site all the way from the raw stage to the built stage, as I personally like both types of sites. I usually have both raw sites 'in the pipeline' (getting approval from council while the development application is in the works) and DA-approved sites already under construction (because I am able to start work on them straight away). This allows a constant flow from one project to the next. By the time one batch of my sites are built, the new raw sites are approved and ready to go.

Those who want to pursue both raw and DA-approved sites will find both on the market, with the DA-approved sites listed in industry advertising. Because a raw site is technically anywhere with potential, however, these are everywhere around you.

In the next chapter you will learn how to find such undeveloped treasures.

CHAPTER THREE:
Finding Your Own Site

" *Property development is not a get-rich-quick industry; you get rich through dedication, contacts and experience.* "

CHAPTER THREE: FINDING YOUR OWN SITE

Part of the excitement of real estate is that you live by your wits. This element of risk and adventure isn't for everyone, but anyone willing to do the research and legwork will reduce their risk and increase the profits that will roll in – a huge motivating factor.

I am always amazed by misleading statements from property gurus and real estate seminar leaders claiming, "I made $150,000 in three weeks by doing such and such a property deal". On paper, yes, it may have taken three weeks, but in reality the person in question had to learn about the business, knock on countless doors, and try and fail on previous deals to get to the point where he or she could snap up a quick deal like that.

Don't be fooled by marketing pitches and crazy claims in property development. It's not a get-rich-quick industry; you get rich through dedication, contacts and experience. And that's the good news – you do a lot of groundwork, yes, but when it does pay off, you get immense financial rewards for your hard work and investment.

In the real estate world, no one will tell you where the good deals are or bring a property that will instantly increase your net worth by a million dollars to your door. There are good – no, *great* – deals out there, but you have to go out and find them yourself. I'm living proof that this works. Here's how.

> **"I have never bought a development site from a real estate agent, there are better ways!"**

RESEARCH TOOLS

Google Maps

Getting an overview of an area is about more than just finding an address. Google Maps can tell you a lot about a location at a glance. You'll see where the site is positioned in relation to parks, hospitals, train stations, post offices, shopping areas, schools and universities – all the things that draw potential buyers and tenants to an area.

You'll see if a piece of property is on a noisy main road or a quiet street far from the main thoroughfare, a short walk from the beach or a car ride away – all elements that change a site's value by hundreds of thousands of dollars or more. Always scan the map for every symbol and detail that adds to your composite picture. This will soon become second nature.

On an aerial map you can see the built-up areas and those that could potentially be built up, and use this information to look into the zoning and future zoning of a particular area to see whether you can target it for development.

Now switch from map view to satellite view. This is one step closer to reality, beyond graphic representation to a photographic, aerial view that fills in a lot of extra visual detail. It is immediately apparent how leafy the streets are or how large the public spaces, how large or small the blocks are, whether the houses and townhouses have gardens or not, and what the minimum subdivision is. In many cases you can even switch to street view and 'drive' up and down the street. Doing so, you might catch a massive electrical structure next door to a site – that's a deal-breaker, and you've just saved yourself some time that you can now use to look elsewhere.

Real Estate Websites

Follow the listings regularly in your areas of interest on:

- www.domain.com.au
- www.realestateview.com.au
- www.realestate.com.au
- www.realestateworld.com.au

And individual agency websites like www.prdnationwide.com.au to get a general feel for how much one-, two- and three-bedroom units in other developments cost, so that you can calculate how much *your* final product will be worth.

Always look at comparable properties – what are other properties in the area selling for *today?* Don't assume any capital gain; that's just a bonus. You need to be able to add value regardless of what the market subsequently does.

Check out www.colliers.com.au, a resource with valuations and management advice. You can also take a look at www.realestateworld.com.au, which highlights trends in the suburb of your choice.

Here are some other websites worth investigating:

Development-Friendly Sites

www.sitesforsale.com.au

www.commentpropertygroup.com.au
(focuses on Queensland)

www.justdevelopmentsites.com.au

www.sharpprojectmanagement.com.au

www.pricefinder.com.au

Businesses/Commercial Sites for Sale

www.realcommercial.com.au

www.bestbusinessbuyes.com.au

www.commercialrealestate.com.au

Australian Property Monitors (apm.com.au) and RESIDEX (residex.com.au) are also good sources for site information, but now let me give you my personal favourite.

RPData.com

Last, but most definitely not least, rpdata.com is the bible of Australian and New Zealand property valuation, offering:

- The values of comparable properties that have recently sold in an area. This goes beyond what prices vendors are asking, which can be wildly unrealistic, and informs you of the prices they accepted – the actual selling prices of the properties.

- The street frontage (width) and size of a block in square metres.

- The time and price of a property's last sale. You can see how the property's value has risen over the years, and also ascertain whether the current owner has owned it for decades or just months. Sometimes a long-term owner is an advantage, as their original buy-in price was so much lower than the current market value that your offer will sound fantastic, even after shaving off 10 per cent or more to buy in low. If, however, someone has just bought recently and overpaid, this could indicate that they need to bail out quickly as they have overcommitted financially. It's always good to know as much as possible about where your vendor is coming from.

- The owner's details. This can be invaluable if you want to make an offer on a property that is not listed for sale, or even assess the future intentions of neighbouring owners.

Agents

Agents are not only the gatekeepers to billions of dollars' worth of property, they are also a goldmine of insider knowledge because they eat, breathe and live the property game.

Pick their brains! Get familiar with calling local agents who have listings in your preferred area and start asking questions.

- How many square metres is the property? (This is essential as a starting point to assess value.

- Why is the owner selling?

- Is he or she negotiable on price?

- What are all of the running costs like council rates?

- Will the owner consider alternative financing methods such as JV, option, and vendor financing. (More on these in Chapter Six.)

- What else is the agent selling right now in a similar range? Leverage the agency contact listed on one property to find out about all the other properties he or she represents. Find out more about his or her current clients and what they are looking for. (Think, who are your competitors?)

Ask them plenty of general questions too, like, "What is moving quickly and what is harder to budge?" and "Where is the next hot spot, and the neighbouring one that will rise after that?" Plus, run through every item on your developer checklist with them (see Chapter Five).

> *"A person who asks questions is a fool for a very short time. A person who doesn't ask questions stays a fool for the rest of their life."*

There are many ways to identify properties worth viewing. Visit the offices and look at all their flyers, 'to lease' and 'to buy' signs – it's like taking the pulse of the neighbourhood. Agents always add 10 to 15 per cent of negotiation 'padding' onto the price, so deduct that and you have an idea of where the market is.

Agents like serious and constant buyers because they keep the whole engine running – and make commissions appear faster. If you let a good agent know that you plan to be trading in property for years to come and will always look at a good deal, you will represent many potential commissions for them. It will be in their interest to look after you, giving you first look at properties not yet on the market and keeping in touch about the next potential hot spot. Even though their job is to represent the vendor, it doesn't hurt to have a friendly rapport with the local agencies.

Look to the Future

One of the ways to find a great site is to do some research on what is happening in the short- to medium-term future. Get an understanding of what types of people are moving into a suburb, and what their needs and wants will be. Sometimes an area is going in a very different direction and this will hugely impact existing values, turbo-charging normal capital gain. When this happens, you want to ride that boom early. Here are some questions to get you started.

- Is a light industrial area about to be rezoned as residential and mixed-use?

- Will people spill over from a neighbouring suburb that has just shot up in value and priced everyone out?

- Is a new hospital being built that will draw new staff to the area? Where will the visitors get a coffee or a meal nearby?

- Are any brothels or noisy nightclubs leaving or coming to the area due to new laws?

- Is a new main road being built that will allow commuters to live here and travel further for work?

- Is an overhead bridge going up?

- Is the infrastructure for a new train line being built?

- What will the existing building site become? An office block bringing in new workers? A shopping centre bringing in shoppers and adding value to existing real estate values?

New Roads

If you go to the State Road and Planning authorities, you can check on all regional and urban projects, light rail proposals, new roads and road outlets. Buying acreage in an area that will have light rail or new roads built through it creates an absolute boom because this means the land will be approved for subdivisions and cheap housing.

Here's where to check this out for each state.

Victoria: www.vicroads.vic.gov.au/Home/RoadProjects/

New South Wales: www.rta.nsw.gov.au/constructionmaintenance/index.html

Western Australia: www.planning.wa.gov.au

South Australia: www.transport.sa.gov.au/transport_network/

Northern Territory: www.nt.gov.au/transport/ntroads/index.shtml

Queensland: www.tmr.qld.gov.au/

Council Websites

This is a great source for envisioning what an area will look like in 10 years' time. Governments move slowly so the council will have already documented its vision for an area over the next decade. There is so much free information about planning, zoning changes, proposed cultural events and future public space. Any major development in the works will be on record as a development application.

Marinas are something to look out for, as they attract wealthy boat lovers who will only live near a berth. If a marina were going to be built within five years, I would invest in that suburb. If something important like this is happening, there will be some trace of it at council.

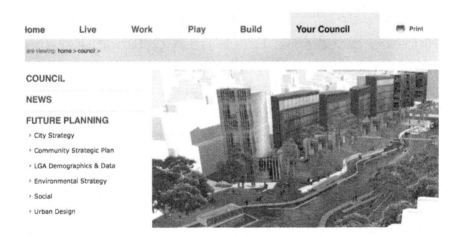

Council plans

PIGGY-BACK ON OTHER PEOPLE'S RESEARCH

It is always useful to see where the big boys are investing – giant chains like hardware outlets, Bunnings, or McDonalds, that omnipotent purveyor of fast foods. Believe me, they have spent millions of dollars in professional research to find out where the population is going to grow, and they do a lot of planning and profit projections before committing to an area. Why not find out where they are investing next?

Following the lead of massive companies can give you more than the external information that they have uncovered about demographics and population flow. When companies like Woolworths, Coles and Stockland set up shop, they make a massive difference to an area afterwards.

High-end grocers like Fratelli Fresh or Simon Johnson always anticipate the new, trendy hot spots, full of urban professionals willing to pay though the nose for imported olive oil and café brunch (along with mid-20th century designer furniture). They, in turn, lift the neighbourhood by their very presence. Any developer who can snap up a site in the next Danks St (a Sydney inner-city oasis of urban chic in the middle of gritty, industrial Waterloo) is sitting pretty.

It's not just about incoming infrastructure. A good property developer learns how to *anticipate*.

If you see a lot of new units going up near a strip of small, dilapidated shops, it is logical to conclude that a lot more people are going to be buying from that corner store beyond the usual 20 houses, and it won't accommodate the area's population in the future. You start to ask the right questions:

- What needs to be bigger?

- What needs to be added?

- What problem needs to be solved?

- What can I do to solve it?

In this case, a mixed-use block of shops at the bottom and apartments on the top would suit the area very well. The shops would accommodate the existing development in the works, and the new apartments would boost the shops even further, providing more customers for potential commercial tenants.

It's all about visualising the future needs of the neighbourhood.

SEE A LOT OF PROPERTIES

This is a numbers game. Developers do not go out and look at one site to find that perfect deal. The more properties you look at, the better chance you have of unearthing the diamond in the rough – and the more you'll know what that is in the first place. You have to hone your skills and go comparison-shopping. If you find a site priced, say, 20 per cent higher than 10 sites just like it – and know that one of the lower-priced ones is much better – you are in a stronger position to pounce on the 'best in show'.

Bottom line: If you can be perfectly happy cruising around town looking for great deals, then you have the makings of a successful property investor or property developer.

Look at a lot of what's selling or has potential and you will come across more gems *and* develop a nose for finding bargain properties. If you haven't looked at 100 properties, how will you know what is good and what is not?

By the time you have looked at 10 properties, you will start to get a pretty specific idea as to what you are looking for.

By the time you have looked at 20 properties, you will start to get a feel for what constitutes a good investment.

By the time you have looked at 50 properties, you may be getting excited about the few that were almost good enough for you to buy.

Keep this process up, and by the time you have looked at 100 properties, you will be surprised by what you have found and what you have learned.

> *"Finding a deal is a numbers game."*

NEVER SWITCH OFF

People drive down the same streets every day and whizz by potentially great development sites – because they are oblivious and don't have a trained eye. If you practice looking for good properties, like anything else, you will get good at it and start to see opportunities everywhere.

I spot development sites just driving around on my way to somewhere else because I have developed an eye for it. I'll see a house on a corner block on a big block of land and automatically start scanning to see how many square metres the neighbouring houses are built on. If that corner house is on, say, double the size of the other lots with twice the street frontage (width) or depth, my brain lights up. You could subdivide and put *two* houses on that site – a potential unit block. Now you're talking!

"Opportunity creates profits – find an opportunity!"

Anyone can develop this knack once they develop the enthusiasm. Ever drive the streets with a vintage car freak? They will spot every GTS Monaro V8 or Valiant Charger and scream with delight. Their eye is so educated and sensitive that if there is a vintage Mustang in the vicinity they'll spot it instantly, and they may even hear it coming.

Similarly, if you stay *constantly curious and calculating,* your new property wisdom will pay off around the clock. Once you understand the rules and regulations of development planning, you see how they can be used to your advantage.

You look, for example, at the potential setbacks (how many metres the building has to be from the street), solutions to problems (where basement parking could fit) and what the minimum land subdivision is. If you know automatically, say, how many metres of frontage are needed in a particular area, then you'll gleefully look for anything substantially bigger. **When you're on a treasure hunt, the treasure leaps out at you.**

TALK TO THE LOCALS

This is my secret weapon. Sure, you may find it intimidating at first, but that's how I was able to find sites that weren't even on agents' radars and be better informed about what was out there than anyone else. I did all my first property deals just talking to the locals – not one single agent was involved in any of them. I personally have taken many of my clients door-knocking to get them started and feel their way. The knowledge you gain by doing this is a great asset!

Locals Are a Great Source of Information

Locals love to gossip. They take pride in their territory and their knowledge about it. They might welcome the chance to air a grievance, or they may just be flattered that someone is interested in what they have to say.

And boy, am I interested! You should be, too.

Once I chatted with a local who lived in the same street as the block that I had come to see. She idly mentioned, "Oh, yeah, there is a bigger road being built through the area, adding another two lanes each way. The council is taking a metre out of all our front lawns". Funny that the real estate agent forgot to tell me that. *Next!*

Another time, a blank lot of land sat across the road from an investment property I was looking at buying, so I asked the locals in a nearby shop if they knew what was happening. They told me there were DA-approved plans for high-density low-cost housing, to go across the road. This would keep a huge permanent lid on the surrounding real estate values, and it killed my interest in the deal.

The 'buyer beware' rule means that it is *your* responsibility to research the area and whatever is outside the parameters of the contract. If you don't research the bigger picture – tough. The agent sure isn't going to reveal anything negative that he or she is not obliged to! The industry policy is 'don't ask, don't tell' – and hope that the buyer doesn't do their research when there is some sticky information around the corner. This is why, as a buyer, you must do your research!

Homeschool

Local homeowners know so much valuable information that you won't hear from any other sources. They can tell you that it is quite noisy on Saturdays when the trucks do their deliveries to the local supermarkets, that the lights from the nearby baseball stadium are very bright at night or that many more families have been moving into the area than singleton flatmates. They know who just moved in, what they paid and whether the price was too high or too low. They have first-hand knowledge about whether it's hard to find tenants or whether you can't rent houses out quickly enough.

I started my career in real estate by finding out exactly these kinds of things right out on the street. My focus was Northmead, which is on the outskirts of Parramatta, the 'other' hub in the western suburbs of Sydney, far from the beaches. At that time Parramatta was affordable, growing in leaps and bounds and still undervalued. Northmead was on the brink of becoming a new town in itself because Parramatta was growing so fast. I knew it was on the verge of explosive short-term growth and I wanted in.

I knocked on doors in Northmead and spoke to more than 100 homeowners, acquiring mountains of information about the demographics of the area – what types of people were already there or moving in, what the future developments were, the efficiency of public transportation, and the exciting infrastructure planned for the near future. I was *all over* Northmead by the time I decided to buy there, accessing the word-of-mouth information that helped me calculate whether I wanted to pursue property there or not.

Locals don't hold back on the details – and they tell you the truth because unlike selling agents, they are unbiased and have no agenda.

In the end I did over five property development deals in this area alone.

"Close the computer and get out on the streets and start talking to people to find deals, you won't believe the amazing opportunities you can put together."

Locals Are Homeowners

If you are willing to do the legwork and talk to the people who live in an area, you could get more than information – you could score a great purchase!

Neighbours often know what will be for sale before it is officially listed, or who is even just thinking about selling. It could be old Bob next door who is going to move out this year because he needs the support of a nursing home, or that lovely couple down the road who are about to have a second child and need a bigger house.

My very first property purchase came together this way. I had done the rounds and spoken to many homeowners, driving through my area and door-knocking. I came across a dilapidated old house and knocked on the door, telling the nice elderly gentleman who answered that I was interested in buying his house. I left him my details, as I had at many other properties, but this time he called me back! We brokered the deal privately. The homeowner wanted to sell the house, which was on a 600-square-metre block, for $230,000. I talked him down $20,000, doing a deal on the phone and agreeing to buy the house for $210,000.

I naturally seek out 'tired properties' like this because they are often a cheap way to get land and the owners can be very motivated to sell. These are not house-proud owners in love with their showcase homes. But you may have more trouble finding the owner if the house is either rented or empty. Don't worry – there are ways to do this and I will discuss how later in the book.

How to Talk to the Locals

 Start small and just practice talking to strangers in your own neighbourhood. Stick to everyday small talk, practicing the art of light, unobtrusive banter and learning how to break the ice. Talk to whoever is accessible, out watering their gardens or checking for mail, and you will soon discover that once you give people a platform to do all the talking, they love the attention and the chance to share about life in their little corner of the world.

When you approach people in the area that you are interested in, don't think of it as cold calling, but as a casual chat. Catching someone in a front garden is always ideal, but you will eventually have to door-knock.

Here's how to make it less confrontational for you – *make it less confrontational for them.* Always be respectful of their space by being as unobtrusive as possible. Here are some additional guidelines.

- **Never stand right at the door after you knock, but take five steps back.** It is the homeowner's call to invite you into their personal space right by the door, and they usually do. If a homeowner beckons you closer and you want to get invited inside, start wiping your feet on the mat. It acts as a subconscious trigger to invite someone across the threshold. (Always be careful for your safety – this is your number-one priority! Don't enter a home or building if you feel unsafe or ill at ease.)

- **Always start off with a reassurance that you are not selling anything, demanding money** or doing anything that will disturb someone in the peace and quiet of his or her own home. "Hi, so sorry to disturb you. My husband and I were just looking in the area" is a nice way to start. There is something innocuous about a young married couple that people can relate to. Then you can ask, "Do you know of anything that's for sale? We just want a house in the area". Which you do! Or say "We are looking for a potential development site," then you could go into what it is you do and offer.

- **Try asking for help.** It's a good way to be less pushy. Say something like, "Hi could you help me? I was looking for a house that was for sale on this street - do you happen to know which one it is? I really want to buy a house on this street; I love it here". People are flattered and proud to be asked for information when they're in the know. From these simple enquiries I have flushed out upcoming sales – and sometimes you'll even pique their own curiosity as to what you would offer them for *their* home!

- **Keep the follow-up questions light and indirect.** People will open up so much more if you sound pleasantly curious rather than downright nosy. Instead of asking the property owner, "How long have you lived here? What do you like or dislike about the area?" lead in with indirect questions like, "This is a great area, have you gotten to know it well? Do people live in the area a long time?" Maybe you'll get lucky with a reply such as, "Yes I have been here for more than 20 years but my husband and I are looking to retire and downsize in a year or two". Perfect! A year or two will give you time to do your homework and get your development application underway.

- **Always make it clear that you are not a real estate agent** (but only if you're not, of course.) For a homeowner, one of the great advantages of selling directly to you is that they don't have to pay an agency commission - 1.5 to 2.5 per cent of the total sales price on average, which can add up to thousands. They also save on marketing costs, which can be as high as $6000 or more. Also, many people simply find dealing directly with the buyer to be a nicer and friendlier way to sell their property, especially if you become friends with them (which I have done on many of my purchases). From your point of view, the advantage is that you don't have an agent playing you off another customer to drive the price up. This is why I actually prefer buying directly.

- **Make it clear that you are a serious potential buyer.** Always leave in a pleasant way, stating your clear interest in buying in the area now or in the near future. You never know, they could start chatting and get someone else interested, or start thinking about selling themselves.

- Simply put, buying directly can be a great way to acquire property, even before a real estate agent becomes aware. Neighbourhood 'one-on-ones' like this are one of my secret property-buying weapons. If there is anyone keen in the street, you can flush out the deal first. There is so much to learn about door-knocking, chatting to the locals and methods of negotiation that I spend a good many hours on this topic in my 'Leverage Academy' events.

I have found this topic to be a highlight at my programs, and the cause for heaps of laughter when I role play this topic. I take students step by step through the process that has been a secret weapon to my success in buying off market properties. This is where you can reap big profits.

CHAPTER FOUR:
Choosing Your Site

" I would rather buy a property in a dirty back alley than a glamorous street because I know that I can utterly transform the look of the area, reaping profits that no one else can see. "

CHAPTER FOUR: CHOOSING YOUR SITE

After you have taken the first steps on your journey to being a property developer – internet research, driving around, talking to local agents and residents – it is time to spread your wings, get a feel for what constitutes a good site and choose your first one.

As with all aspects of property development, there is both a general mindset to maintain and a list of specific things to consider. Remember, this is business and you are looking for a deal from the standpoint of up-front profit. You're a developer in the making who is thinking about profits *now*, not a starry-eyed residential buyer looking for your dream nest for the next 25 years. That's who you *sell* to.

> *"You make your money when you buy, not when you sell, with clear profits up front. You simply extract them at the end."*

THE 'THINK PROFITABLE, NOT PRETTY' MINDSET

That blue-ribbon suburban street may be the first choice for emotional buyers willing to pay inflated prices, and you may even love the look of it yourself. But don't let the moss-covered sandstone or glorious song of the neighbourhood bluebirds seduce you into thinking, 'I gotta have it!' Once you put pen to paper and do the figures, you may find the in-cost so prohibitive that there is simply no profit to be had. In fact, you might find that you'd actually take a loss in any development deal. So leave those properties for other investors or homeowners.

I would rather buy a property located in a dirty back alley than a glamorous street because I know that I can utterly transform the look of the area, reaping profits that no one else can see by enhancing the appeal of the whole street with a fantastic new block of units.

I have made a lot of my money in property by buying in what most people would consider the worst possible locations, when in fact they are *great* locations for adding new real estate, making profits and lowering your risk. Property development is not always about the prettiest block or suburb or how a site looks or feels.

The numbers are the only thing that should get you excited or make you scrap the deal.

When it comes to selling a property, being near shops, schools, public transport and train stations is great, and a nice park can be helpful, but being in the most glamorous street isn't essential. To a developer, a 'good location' does not mean a posh spot but a profitable one.

DEVELOPER CHECKLIST

As I mentioned, there are also specific factors that any developer must consider when looking at a raw site that, to the naked eye, seems to have potential. Remember that as a property developer, the buck stops with you – you must check absolutely *everything.* The council, agents and owners will not come knocking to volunteer this information! It is up to you to do your due diligence.

THE DEVELOPER CHECKLIST I AM ABOUT TO GIVE YOU IS THE BEDROCK OF MY OWN SITE RESEARCH.

A draftsman and a town planner can help you inspect a site with potential if you feel out of depth in these matters. This is worth the investment if you want to fully understand the situation and what is required of you.

Council Investigations and Make-Your-Own Investigations

Many properties ripe for development can be cherry-picked just by driving around, but it is equally important to avoid the pitfalls and dodge the sites that you should not buy, no matter how appealing they are on first look.

Zoning. Check with council to determine the current and/or future zoning on the property, which will give you the boundaries on what types of building are permitted.

Floor Space Ratio (FSR). This is the ratio of a building's floor area to the land the building sits on. It provides a guide as to how much floor area can be built on a particular parcel of land.

Setbacks. These vary by zoning districts, and will stipulate the distance that a new building must be set back from the property boundaries.

149 Certificate or Zoning Certificate. This includes the type of land zoning (for example, 'Residential R2') as well as whether it is affected by floods, bushfires, road widening, etc. Before you buy a property, it's essential to have a recent copy of this.

SQM and Boundaries. One of the first things to take a look at is a property's total square metres (or 'SQM'). You should also look at its frontage and depth, and whether it is a weird or unusable shape. I always start by stepping out the boundaries to get a rough calculation of the area and looking over the fence to see the land itself. Then I go to more accurate sources to determine the exact SQM because, like any development under council regulations, there must be a certain amount of SQM and frontage to get a development application through. If this is the case, you might need to look at more land and amalgamating the properties.

Shadowing. Where does the sun come up and set? A north-facing residence is generally considered most desirable as it gets the morning sun, hence more natural light. It is also more protected from the colder southerly winds. The aspect is important.

Trees. Are there any big trees on the property? You may have a fabulous 2000-square-metre development site but have to build around the massive oak tree slap bang in the middle that you might not be allowed to remove. Sometimes you can find useful solutions. For instance, if the property has smaller trees, reuse them elsewhere on the site or sell them to a nursery to help offset your costs. Some councils require permission.

Asbestos. Always be aware of the presence of asbestos, as you have to factor in a higher cost for its removal when demolishing.

Easements. An easement is where water escapes – it's an absolute physical necessity. An easement always needs to be either publicly accessible or encased at a cost if you are allowed to build over part of it. Easements can be deal-breakers, so do your homework!

Slope. Does the land lean toward the gutter, or have a significant slope? A gradual slope toward the gutter is ideal, because water will easily run off into the street. But a significant slope will mean higher construction costs. So do the numbers and find out what's feasible. You may find yourself in a position to negotiate for more off the buy price to offset the increased development costs. Keep in mind that water must run off somewhere – maybe through a neighbouring property. Take into consideration that you may have to pay the neighbour to use their backyard as an easement. If the neighbour refuses unreasonably, the council may be able to make them give you access, but if the refusal is for a valid reason then you can be stopped from building on that site.

Flood Zone. Is the property in a zone that is easily flooded? This will have a big impact on how feasible it is to build on the site, as you may be denied permission to build at all. If you are permitted to build, you may have to do so on stilts. The potential of flooding will also determine whether you can build basement parking and what will be required if you do. All of this can have a big impact on your numbers and your return, so check it out.

Geotech Report. If you are excavating to build basement parking, you'll need a geotech report – an expert analysis of the physical land you want to build on that will reveal any unseen but potentially expensive problems. The ground could be contaminated (a common problem with old petrol stations), and the high cost of fixing this would need to be factored in. Or there could be solid rock under the ground, which costs a fortune to get rid of and has caused many a development to come undone.

Caveats on the Property. A caveat, which technically means a warning or caution, asserts certain statutory rights on a property by another party (the beneficiary of a will, for example) other than the registered landowner. This means the other party's interests encumber the land and the new owner will not have total control. As caveats only appear on original Certificates of Title and not on duplicates, always do a register search of that Certificate of Title itself. Although there are legal ways to remove caveats, this may prove time-consuming and possibly even unsuccessful.

24/7 Noise Levels. Make sure you've walked around the site at different times of the day, from early morning and lunchtime during the week to late at night and during weekend leisure time. You may miss the regular occurrence of crucial neighbourhood noise, like 'Saturday sub-woofer' nightclub sounds, if you always visit at the same time of day. Passing trains and aircraft noise are two other examples. If it is noisy, you may need to get an acoustics sound report engineer to estimate how impactful this will be to life in your building, and therefore your resale figures. The engineer can estimate the need for double-glazed windows at an added cost.

Road Building. You must consult with council as to whether you will be required to add any roads to your development site to accommodate traffic to the area. You should also confirm whether council is carrying out any road-widening in the area that would impact your site. These are not necessarily deal-breakers, but you have to factor them into your decision and decide whether to walk away or forge ahead. Buying may still be well worth it once you've factored the sometimes expensive solutions into your budget – but be aware that *if the price seems too good to be true, it generally is, and a development problem is probably lurking.*

What Other Development Applications Are in Council?

Other developments can impact the feel and value of a potential property, so always make sure that you check at council to see what other DAs have been filed in any area you're thinking about developing.

Will there be construction next door for the next 12 months, making it impossible to rent out the units in your development? Then factor that cost in! Will a childcare centre be going in next door? This will impact the serenity of an otherwise quiet street and create traffic bottlenecks every morning and afternoon.

Is the area growing, with new facilities that will attract more buyers and renters to the area? Good! Are the Hell's Angels building their new headquarters next door? Not so good. It can be hard to sell property near methadone clinics as well, along with anything that gives off bad odours, like an abattoir. Okay, you get the point. Do your homework.

I was once looking at buying some investment units on the beachfront in Narrabeen, on Sydney's northern beaches. I did my due diligence at council to see what other DAs were in, and sure enough, there were *two* unit blocks under development next door that were going to block all my ocean views. This would have wiped value off my own block that would never return. Knowing this, I didn't pursue the deal.

Will There Be an Oversupply (or Undersupply) in the Market Where You Want to Build?

Let's say you've found a site with brilliant potential for building a new block of 30 units. Now imagine learning that a big company like Meriton or Mirvac had gotten in first and were building a massive block of 600 two-bedroom units nearby. They will come on the market and soak up all the incoming buyers. You just can't compete with the budgets or prices of these powerhouse companies, either. So in a case like this, it could be better to walk away.

Investigating other DAs in council can also seal the deal by informing you of what is going to be undersupplied. Maybe an influx of apartments will create a need for a great commercial strip nearby!

CHOOSING WHAT TO BUILD ON YOUR SITE

Deciding what to build is the crucial second phase of choosing a site and putting a deal together. A good developer must think *way* ahead. Two big initial questions are part and parcel of choosing the right site.

Question 1 - Who will I be selling the finished product to?

You are not just buying a piece of land; you are buying into a neighbourhood. So who will want to live there when your development work is done? You need to have a clear picture of your buyer in mind – the most feasible buyer for that location and apartment.

Just as it's crucial to get the right buy-in price at the beginning, it's just as important to make sure you can sell (or rent, if that's the strategy) when you're finished building. Work out who you will be selling to first. Preferably, this will be a gap in the demographic not being adequately catered to right now.

Are you building townhouses for an overseas market? For example some people prefer gas over electric cooking, no graveyard within a loud 'cooee' of the development, and ditch the number four (it is unlucky and use good feng shui).

Is the area popular with ethnic families who want a massive entertaining area for the 20 family members who turn up on the weekend for a barbeque? Uni students who just need one bedroom? Funky urban young couples who need a media centre in a big office space but never eat in and won't care much about the kitchen? Work out who your most likely buyer will be, then cater to their needs.

This is where all your market research comes in. Who lives in the suburb? Who is *aspiring* to move there (i.e., who can you help get a foot in the door)? What services and amenities do they need? What is the main attraction for these buyers – the local community, the birds and trees, or maybe the commuter-friendly railway station?

Where is the council spending money? What does that tell you about the demographic and who the council most expects to migrate to the area?

Here's a real-life example of a DA-approved site that came across my radar recently. It shows how the needs of the market can define whether a site is interesting or not, even when the numbers stack up promisingly.

Some colleagues and I found an awesome site that had been approved by council, and we calculated that we would turn a good profit. However, the site had a partial over-55 living requirement, i.e. a certain number of dwellings must provide exclusive availability for someone in that age range.

That in itself wasn't the problem. The problem was that the only type of building approved on the DA for this site was four to five-bedroom homes. This would have really limited our target market, and therefore resale. Our 55-or-older buyers for these homes would have to be in big families where they would live with their adult children – quite rare in Australian culture. Most of the buyers this law is designed to provide for are mainly looking for single-storey villas, with two bedrooms and safety aids like handles in the bathtub. They don't want big two-storey houses. Yes, we might have found other ethnic groups who might have gone for these homes, but instead of taking three months to sell, they could have taken six months or more, leading to spiralling holding costs (mainly in the form of interest payments to the bank that financed the deal).

When you choose a raw site, you have to anticipate and build for the market that is out there. And if you're looking at a DA-approved site, make sure that the plans already consider the same thing. Avoid sites that appeal to a too-limited target market with niche requirements.

Question 2 – How much will I be selling my finished product for?

Always create properties on your site that will service the widest part of the bell curve – where the majority of buyers are and will be if the market takes a hit. I always recommend creating a development site that is not priced at the very top end of the market in that area, but at the most popular and affordable end. Catering for the mass of people in any given area gives you more room to move if the market takes a downturn, and a wider future client base competing with each other if it booms.

For example, in a market range of $750,000 to over $1 million, a lot can go wrong if you start tailoring to the top customer. If the market changes even slightly, your glamorous triplexes could be worth less and less. But even if the market drops a bit, you'll always be able to sell your $550,000 units because this is the average price range for that type of suburb – these properties will always be in demand and affordable. And if the market takes a hit, this can even create *more* demand for your affordable housing in pricey areas. It's a win-win for everyone involved and it lowers your risk.

So when looking for a suitable raw site, always factor in whether or not you can put the maximum amount of good quality, affordably priced sites there. Ask yourself how much risk is involved in the site.

If you tick all the boxes in this chapter, you'll have a rock-solid foundation for what is to come.

CHAPTER FIVE:
The 'F' Word — Feasibility

" *I must have saved people millions over the years with a simple pen, napkin and calculator! Property development is very capital-intensive, and you have to get your sums right.* "

CHAPTER FIVE: THE 'F' WORD – FEASIBILITY

Every stage in the process thus far, from embarking on the journey to passive income and undreamt-of profits to hunting down the deals, is the fun part of the development process.

I see how the prospect of creating wealth out in the field and juggling deals inspires my students every time I run a course. But they usually come unstuck at the feasibility stage, when they have to test the true worth of a deal. Property development is an adventurous treasure hunt that brings you riches and free time – yippee! But to get there, you have to get serious about the number-crunching.

My students and clients come to me all the time in a lather of excitement, taking the word of a real estate agent and running with them, or falling in love with a site in their favourite area. "Fantastic," I'll say. "Let's jot down the numbers and do a quick feasibility right now."

When I work out the sums in even the most cursory, general way, I often see that the profit margin is far too narrow, or even in doubt, and that the deal is not worth pursuing unless many aspects of it change. I must have saved people millions over the years with a simple pen, napkin and calculator!

Property development is very capital-intensive, and you have to get your sums right. If you miscalculate your costs and/or profit margin, that one mistake flows through every other calculation. You could even end up in arrears on a deal that you thought would be lucrative.

Part of the excitement of real estate is that you live by your wits. This element of risk and adventure isn't for everyone, but anyone willing to do the research and legwork will reduce their risk and increase the profits that will roll in – a huge motivating factor.

Do the research and work the numbers – and only proceed if they come up trumps, no matter what!

Don't be in such a hurry to nail a deal that you think might slip through your fingers that you skip the necessary research and feasibility study. I have had the privilege of meeting Frank Lowey, the co-founder of the

Westfield Shopping Centre empire and currently at pole position on the *Business Review Weekly* list of Australia's richest men. Now I'll share his sage advice with you.

Lowey told me his simple golden rule is this: **Don't rush in.**

Here's what he said in a bit more detail. They're worth committing to memory. "Libby, never regret the deals that you don't do, because there is always another, even better deal just around the corner. Never be in a rush to buy for the sake of it!"

In property, if you get it wrong, you can wind up with a headache and a money pit that can last for years. So let's make sure that never happens to you and that you master the crucial feasibility stage before even considering the next step.

A basic feasibility study involves the following aspects:

- Buy price

- Buying costs

- Holding costs

- Development application costs

- Council fees

- Consultant fees

- Build costs

- Selling agents fees.

Note that this is a basic outline for a feasibility study. There is a lot more detail involved in these costs, and we study this process in depth in my 'Leverage Academy' program.

> **"You must bring all the pieces of the puzzle together to make the development site work. If one piece is wrong it could all fall apart."**

THE CRITICAL STEPS OF THE FEASIBILITY PROCESS

Know How Much Your Stock Will Sell For

This is your starting point, because the only income you have coming in on a development site is sales – if you get that wrong, you get the whole thing wrong. A good developer *has* to check for feasibility and be realistic about the selling price.

This is where the novice often comes unstuck. I can't tell you how many rookies have come to me excited about a deal, but when I ask the crucial question, "What is the resale price?" they airily reply, "Oh, probably around $550,000 each" when there is a massive difference between each unit in a block of 30 units!

Instead, I want to hear a solid resale figure based on recent sales from RPData.com and lots of agent feedback. You really need to be detailed and realistic on resale. And conservative! Don't even factor capital gains into your calculations, as this is a huge maybe. What's the sure thing? What could you get for it *today*? If you get good capital growth over the 12 months, that's a bonus, but don't ever get cocky and factor it in ahead of time.

One very experienced developer mentor of mine refers to his units for resale as 'stamps' – they have a set worth, and for the time being, it is what it is. You are selling stamps, not art. Make sure you are comparing apples with apples!

Once I get really serious about buying a development site I will sit down and go through each and every unit, factor in how many bedrooms it will have, its square metres, aspect, level, view, whether it will have one or two car spaces, etc. Then I will create a resale figure for each one of the 30 units individually. I actually love doing this! But the key point is that it's necessary.

Don't Take Someone Else's Word

How many people lose money in an unprofitable deal and then say, "But Jack said it was a good buy and it was going to go up in value really soon".

Why was the value meant to go up? Because Jack said so? You need a rationale behind every assertion (or hope) about the future; you need to dissect the deal on the table for yourself. Never trust anyone else's word, no matter how nice and sincere they are. Real estate agents, for example, will have a vested interest – if they are selling a potential development site, of course they will talk up how much apartments are going for in the area. A competitor could be trying to lead you astray. Neighbours, friends, family members and fellow developer may erroneously tell you that a property is a good buy for any number of reasons – and genuinely believe it.

No matter their reason, if other people have it wrong then *you* will be the one to lose – not only money in that deal, but also the opportunity cost of *not* having that money in another great deal.

Take information from other people into account, but always double-check it with independent sources, especially when the information comes from people who have nothing to do with the site and no commission at stake in your buying the property. Check the say-so of others against hard data, such as recent sales on RPData.com. If it is your name on the dotted line, or you are the one bringing co-investors on board – the final responsibility lies with no one but you.

Research! Research! Research!

You need to know how this deal will turn out right to the final stage. You should be asking:

- How can I structure it to maximize my profits?

- How can I get it for as little money down as possible?

- How can I hold on to it for as long as possible without paying money?

Bargains are great. We love bargains. And I discuss the good reasons why a property could be a bargain in Chapter Seven. But a site may be a bargain for some bad reasons, too. Ask yourself why the seller is getting rid of it. Beware of a bargain, but snap it up if it's good!

FEASIBILITY ON DA-APPROVED SITES

DA-approved sites are valuable because all this research and groundwork has been done. That's why you get great returns for taking a raw site and turning it into land with the council go-ahead; a developer can just get building.

But even with a DA-approved site, you still have to do your feasibility to see if the plan that has been pre-approved will work for *you*.

Look Carefully at the DA

Look for any DA issues or unpredictable construction issues. Is there a really intricate roof design or fancy cantilevered (overhanging) pool that will add a huge expense and nightmare complexity for the builder, tiler, plumber or electrician? Are there lifts, and if so, how many? Is there a single or a double basement? You want to know exactly what you are getting into.

What is the DA's Shelf Life?

An approved development application is typically valid for five years. If it expires before you commence the building, the zoning may have changed, limiting what you can then construct.

Has the Construction Certificate Been Completed?

A construction certificate is legally required after the council has given consent for development but before building or subdivision can occur. It outlines everything from the site preparation, to the specific structural materials and finishes including landscaping plans.

Have the Council Contributions Been Paid?

Council contribution fees are for local roads, parks, libraries, trees, etc. As unit block construction attracts more people to an area, the greater population adds a strain on existing services, so the council must be compensated. Find out what, if anything, must be paid and take care of it, as this must be done before construction begins.

FEASIBILITY FACTORS

Every project, whether simple and small, like knocking down a house to build two townhouses, or large and complex, like constructing a block of 20 apartments, needs a feasibility study. Your feasibility study should comprise all the factors that affect the total price of and eventual profit on a deal. By working within its parameters, you can calculate accurately what you can build on any given site and what it will cost.

Selling what you build is where you make your return on property development, so you need to factor in every step right up to the end sale. Only when you know you'll make a good profit at the end does a design become feasible.

Design Feasibility

Architects and draftsmen are able to create the 'design feasibility' for your site so that you can calculate the returns. In the beginning you will need someone else to do this. After many years of doing developments I have learned how to check off what I can put on a site – but I still double-check with my architect.

As a property developer, I find it essential to be able to quickly calculate a project's feasibility myself, as I can run through the numbers and get a rough idea before I proceed any further and engage paid professionals. I have used this skill countless times as an initial green or red light on any project that comes up on my extensive property radar.

You will eventually be able to do this, too. For now, you will be able to look at any site as a developer by first gaining an understanding of the following considerations.

LEP Zoning

A Local Environment Plan (LEP) is the council's legal guide to what land uses are permitted in each zone that the council covers. Clearly, what you can build in a residential zone (dwellings to live in) is different from what you can build in a commercial zone (shops where commerce and trading can occur) or an industrial zone (factories and spaces for manufacturing goods). Each zone has its restrictions and prohibited uses.

As styles of building suit different purposes, zoning also extends to specific development standards such as height and density controls. To maintain the character of a historic low-rise residential neighbourhood, for example, there may be a three-storey limit on all unit blocks.

In 2010, some states implemented a more standard LEP template to maintain consistency between councils.

City councils can provide LEP maps that give an immediate overview of several concerns, including:

Land zoning map. This indicates how the land has been zoned. Legal options for building in certain streets vary: residential, townhouses, mixed-use (a combination of business and residential), senior living, commercial, industrial, etc. You can look up or buy zoning maps from the council that will not only inform you about the possibilities of property for sale, but indicate the development-friendly zones where you should be looking.

Lot Size Map. This shows the minimum subdivision area for each lot.

Minimum Lot Size Map for Dual-Occupancy. This shows the minimum subdivision area for each lot for dual-occupancy development.

Height of Building Map. This indicates the maximum height of buildings in metres.

Town Centre Precinct Map and Minimum Site Area Map. This shows the minimum site area for development in town centres.

Floor Space Ratio Map (FSR). This indicates the amount of development area expressed as a ratio of the amount of total site area.

Land Reservation Acquisition Map. This shows any land required for road widening, open space, drainage, or strategic bus corridors.

Environmentally Sensitive Lands Map. This indicates any significant vegetation corridors along creek lines and any other significant pockets of vegetation.

Unstable Land Map and Acid Sulphate Soils Map. This identifies any lands that are too chemically or geologically unstable to build on.

DCP Zoning

A Development Control Plan (DCP) applies the overreaching conditions of the LEP to your particular project in a more detailed manner. Design guidelines include the actual appearance, size and form of whatever you propose building once you have taken the LEP zoning and restrictions into consideration (i.e. the LEP tells you that you have to build a shop in that street; the DCP will have more to do with what that shop should actually look like).

The design objectives and restrictions are usually illustrated by diagrams, and have often been created in tandem with community input. The DCP rules also ensure that you carry out your LEP-friendly development in an environmentally sustainable way.

To get a feel for these documents, you can usually find them on the development pages of your local council website.

Gross Floor Area (GFA). This is the ratio of building to land allowed. A GFA of 50 per cent (in which half the land can be built on) will clearly allow a developer far less end product to sell than a GFA of 90 per cent, which makes nine-tenths of the land available to build on.

Floor Space Ratio (FSR). Technically this measurement is the Gross Floor Area divided by the Site Area – in other words, the total floor area of a building relative to the actual plot. If the FSR is 2.0, then the total area of the floors constructed on the allowed parcel must not exceed twice the size of the parcel itself. This would allow a two-storey construction (if height restrictions also allow). An FSR of 3.0 would let you do three storeys, and so on.

Overall Height Restriction. This tells you the maximum height allowance for the buildings in a particular area.

Construction. Because this is always the biggest cost, developers will hire or consult a professional quantity surveyor for a building quote or a 'QS report' during the decision-making process on whether or not to develop a site.

Another way of doing these figures is to go to either www.bmtqs.com.au or www.reconstruction.com to calculate construction costs per square metre.

Some extra costs that you may need to factor in include:

Lifts. Any new building with more than three stories requires a lift by law. There is a huge cost for each lift, so you can never afford to forget this one in your feasibility study. Lifts can range from $60K-$300K.

Basement Car Park. Most unit and townhouse developments require basement parking, so the amount of car spaces will depend on the amount of units you are adding to the area. If it is a significant enough number and the single-storey basement has to become a double-story basement, this is considerably more expensive. My rough rule of thumb is $15K – $30K per car space for underground car park construction.

Conveyancing. This is the legal process of putting a property on the market, concluding an agreement to sell and buy, and transferring ownership of the property to your purchaser. In other words, it's the legal transaction of buying and selling, which is handled though the legal channels of a lawyer or conveyancer. A lawyer is best equipped to handle more complex legal issues that arise; a conveyancer is usually used for simple transactions and is cheaper.

Finance Establishment Fee. This is the fee charged by the bank for setting up your mortgage, so you can borrow the funds needed to secure the property – one to two per cent of the borrowed amount is the usual fee. Once you establish a relationship with a bank you can negotiate a more exact figure, but in the meantime, err on the conservative side and calculate this at **two per cent.**

Selling Fee. This is charged by the agent who sells the property and commissions vary. If you can convince the agent that he or she will get a lot more business from you than the normal buyer who only sells once every 15 years or so, then negotiate as much off the selling fee as you can. But also remember that great agents pay for themselves because they can get you much better outcomes than bad agents. So always choose the superior agent who gets top dollar for the area or type of property you're selling, even if he or she charges slightly more.

Marketing and Sales Costs. These costs are incurred when you advertise the finished real estate product for sale. A slickly produced advertising campaign is what lures buyers, and this includes brochures, billboards, mail drop-offs, photography and internet advertising. Plan to allocate a percentage of your total proceeds to this.

Stamp Duty. This is charged by the government for each purchase of a site. You can bet that the state taxman gets his due on every purchase, but this can be offset by certain grants. These vary from state to state and with other factors, such as time or whether it is your first purchase. Learn more at www.stampdutycalculator.com.au.

Finance Costs. Borrowing money creates a monthly debt of interest repayments for the life of the loan. These are part of the 'holding costs' of a property – the longer that you hold it without selling, the longer the interest continues to grow. This is why developers often do better deals on 'off the plan' (as yet unbuilt) units, to offset some of this debt.

Council Contributions. When you create a significant population increase within an area due to your development of added residential dwellings, more people will be using the local parks, libraries, footpaths, roads, etc. Some councils require money to contribute toward the upkeep of these local facilities. Your contributions can vary greatly depending on how upmarket or near the city the area is – as an example, anywhere from $5000 to $25,000. This must be paid before construction starts, as part of getting the full construction certificate approved.

Construction Certificate or Building Application. This final approval and sign-off by council so that you can commence building is a paid service.

Demolition. If you need to remove an existing dwelling before you can build, this could cost at least $20,000. If any materials such as asbestos need to be removed carefully, then the quote will be even higher.

Extras. A good read through the DA conditions report will sometimes indicate extra costs that are required on a case-by-case basis, such as water retention tanks. Your feasibility won't be complete until you have studied enough to flush out any of these extras.

Contingencies. This allows some space in your budget for the variables and unforeseen occurrences that are part and parcel of construction – things like hitting a pipe, discovering a weird angle in a basement car park that is generally modelled on a square shape, or anything that ends up costing extra to deal with. It's next to impossible to put a fixed price on things down to the dollar, so **_always assume_** that you will need that extra five per cent of total costs on a straightforward site. For more complex sites, I factor in 10 per cent. Being able to determine a site's potential complexity comes with experience, so assume the worst in your early days as a property developer.

End Profit. This, of course, is the final figure you are aiming at in all your feasibility studies. I seek at least 15 to 20 per cent profit to deem a deal viable, but I like to aim more toward 30 per cent.

MY TIPS FOR THE MOST EFFECTIVE FEASIBILITY STUDIES

- Most importantly, do the figures at the beginning of the project, not the end!

- If the numbers stack up by even five to 10 per cent on a quick feasibility calculation, then work with them and see if you can do something better to nudge your return up to 20 per cent or more. If you can find a way, great – but if you can't, don't be tempted to downplay some negative aspect of the numbers and 'talk down' your feasibility. This is a sure way to lose money.

- Figure out what price you would need to buy the property for the numbers to work, and *stick to that price.*

- If the numbers don't support a profit, or if the figures indicate the project will go over-budget, scrap it and move on to something else.

Don't invest emotionally! Feasibility studies are only about calculating whether you can make a profit for the amount of work you need to put in – it's not about making the unworkable work.

> *"I quit being afraid when I failed my first venture and the sky didn't fall down."*
> *- Allen H. Neuharth*

To access your free webinar
training now, simply go to:

www.LibbyLombardo.com/bonus

0:18 / 7:03 HD

CHAPTER SIX:
DA Day - Getting Development Approval

" This is about dollars and cents, not emotions and mental victory. "

CHAPTER SIX: DA DAY - GETTING DEVELOPMENT APPROVAL

Although many developers look for DA-approved sites, my own experience of launching into the property game was by finding raw sites and adding the initial value to the land. This chapter focuses on taking a piece of land with untapped, unseen potential and adding value from the very beginning.

Raw sites are a great way for beginners – people who often have more time than money – to get into property development.

If you are starting out in the property game, you can get started by finding raw sites just like I did. Once you put the time, energy and comparatively small investment into getting your site DA-approved, you can on-sell it to a bigger, more established developer.

This is a great way to get to the point where you want to make the profits at the other end as well, and oversee the site all the way through to the building stage to gain even bigger profits. Even if you do end up specialising in sites that already have DA approval, you may come across a raw site that is too good to pass up, and you'll have the know-how to get it rubber-stamped by the council.

Either way, it is important to gain mastery in the all-important step of getting council approval for your development application. All hail the DA as a value-adding tool!

TEAM PLAYERS - WHO YOU WILL NEED

Architect

What the architect brings to your development team is part technical skill, part design artistry. You will need the expertise of someone who is used to thinking in the spatial realm. Not only will they be able to confirm what you can feasibly build on a site, they will know how to cleverly maximise the use of the land and solve the challenges of making its visuals work within the council's rules.

The architect also provides working drawings that create a graphic representation of the building. This blueprint will determine the layout and correct measurements of the construction process.

Here's what to look for in an architect:

- Because they are trained to see the potential of space differently, they will offer creative solutions that could add design distinction or legally increase floor space. Architecture is an art, not just a science; it is worth paying for excellence.

- You want an architect with a good, proven track record with council; it may save your DA from going to the bottom of the pile.

- Make sure your architect (or draftsman, if the project is not too big) is willing to inspect the site with you to get a feel for the actual area.

- Look for an architect who communicates quickly and easily with you. You shouldn't have to chase them; it slows down a project at each stage.

- Seek out architects who have experience on similar development projects to yours, whether it's an aged-care facility, a block of chic townhouses or a high-end retail space.

- Ask for references from prior clients and review them.

Quality Surveyor

The role of the quality surveyor, or 'QS', is to provide independent advice on the financial costs of construction and assist in maintaining the budget. Unlike the UK, where the QS has a more accountable role in project management, in Australia the final responsibility to monitor spending and stay on-budget still lies with you, the developer. The QS can tell you what should be happening; you have to make sure it *is* happening.

Town Planner

The town planner works at council. His or her job is to look at all aspects of land use and management in suburban and urban areas and then deduce the optimum use for each parcel of land. They would take into account environmental factors like congestion and pollution, social factors like crime, demographics and recreation, and economic factors like land values and existing legislation.

Developing a cooperative relationship with your town planner is an invaluable way to gain insight into what is coming up in the area and the best way to speed your DA through council. Remember, once you finance a deal, the clock is ticking and you are paying interest.

Libby Lombardo

If you just go to the council's front desk, you will get a junior planner who won't be the best-informed person there. Try to find out who the senior planner is and run your concepts by him or her. It can be very helpful to bounce your ideas off this person, but keep in mind that he or she will be even more forthcoming with a firm opinion once you actually submit your DA.

Engineer

As experts in the physics of design, engineers are able to tell you what is technically possible – and legal – to construct. It is important to have a good working relationship with one because you, the developer, will be required to provide engineer's reports in your DA to guarantee the safety of the project and compliance with council.

YOUR DA CHECKLIST

Development Control Plans

When you submit your DA you will want to get it right to ensure that it will be approved quickly. Go to the council's website and the Development Control Plans will provide you with the guidelines for preparing your application and the conditions that will produce a positive assessment. This will also reveal important information about the suburb.

Land Title Search. Doing a land title search is a necessary step in any property transaction and gives you, the prospective buyer, a legal history of all previous ownership of the land. This ensures that property passes from one hand to another in an orderly, legal fashion and proves that the land is the owner's to sell to you.

Environmental Impact Assessment. This study compiles data and analysis to predict the physical impact of the development, e.g. gas, electrical and water consumption, will have on the surrounding area. Often this is done as part of the town planning process.

Survey Plans. The surveyor will map the dimensions of an individual lot of land, including its size, shape, boundary lines, the distance between certain points and angles and the dimensions of the surrounding lots.

When developers propose new subdivisions of land into lots, they seek separate title over each new lot created, and must submit this to the council as part of their DA application.

As you can see, there are a lot of administrative hoops to jump through, *but that is how you are adding value.* And from experience I can tell that you that it gets exponentially easier every time. Once you have your reliable team of experts lined up, you delegate each task and everyone knows how to do their part.

> *"Become a deal maker, then get the experts to put it all together for you."*

YOUR DA BIBLES

There are two council reference sources that you should purchase, as I did when I did my first deal – the DCP *Development Control Planning Guide* and the LEP *Land and Environment Planning Guide*. They cover, for the council that publishes them:

- the planning policy of that council

- the minor land use changes that are exempt from permission

- the land uses that are allowed in the zone that affects your property

- maximum envelopes of floor space and height

- council policy on heritage and social housing, etc.

Mastering these topics will do a great deal to demystify the process and teach you the council mindset. Once you are willing to take on the administrative work this entails, you can add serious value and start making profit on land.

Tips on Getting Your DA Approved

All of your hard work will be wasted if the council doesn't approve your application in the end, so you should optimise your chances. You need a 'yes' and you need to speed up the process. Here's how.

- **Speak with council first.** If you don't talk to the local council before making a commitment to buy a piece of property, you could get stuck with land that you can't improve. Make sure ahead of time that your 'profitable strategy' isn't a deal-breaker that the council would never approve.

- **Be personal.** Get to know the council and build a relationship with the staff there before you submit your DA so that they can put a face to your name. The business of bricks and mortar still boils down to people working with people, so it's only normal that requests go more smoothly when backed by real, human connection and respect. DAs are more popular and numerous now than ever, and your local council may have two or three town planners and 200 DAs in its in-tray – so be visible and memorable in a positive way.

- **Be easy to deal with.** Be flexible and willing to communicate, and always be respectful of the town planner's time and point of view. He or she is far more likely to give you a positive outcome if you are a pleasure to work with.

- **Show that you will improve the area.** Keep coming back to the reasons why your development is only going to make the council area a better place to live. That is its mandate, so demonstrate how you'll contribute to it.

- **Know your parameters.** Be very clear on zoning restrictions and subdivision rules up front so that you don't waste time making no-go requests.

- **Streamline your DA.** If your DA contains items you suspect or know might stimulate some debate in council or otherwise slow down the approval process, remove them and submit the initial DA so you can get started with construction. Later on, you can submit a subsequent DA or a Section 96 (which modifies the original DA or corrects errors) and deal with the controversial items later.

- **Pre DA meeting.** In a pre-development meeting you can arrange some basic concept images to go over your plans and ideas. You will usually get a clear indication if your concept is on the right track.

What Happens Next

If the council approves your DA, you have permission to build. This is it – you're on your way! You can either on-sell the land at a profit or finance the construction yourself.

If the Development Assessment Commission does not approve your DA, go back and work with the council and your designer to see why. Ascertain what it would take to tweak your DA enough to get approval and then take this route – as long as it is still profitable, of course. This may seem like a real hassle, but it will still take a lot less time and money than ditching the project and starting from scratch.

Remember, this is about dollars and cents, not emotions and mental victory. So take your ego, pride, frustration and anger out of the equation, go back to council and offer to take the DA back to the drawing board. Ask what you can do to make the proposal work and get it over the line. Make sure that the numbers stack up (if you have done your initial feasibility study, they still will) and keep trying until you make it work.

> *"Do your homework, know there is a profit, then go through the step-by-step process to extract the profits."*

CHAPTER SEVEN:
Getting Started with Little or No Money

> *"The one ingredient that true go-getters have, even when they are starting with next to nothing, is a can-do attitude rooted in the determination to find a way – any way – to begin."*

CHAPTER SEVEN: GETTING STARTED WITH LITTLE OR NO MONEY

Believe it or not, it is possible to get started in the property development game with little or no money – my students are always surprised by this. Let me show you how it's done.

Here are the tools (what I think of as 'secret weapons') you will need to think bigger than you look on paper – and start with little or no money down.

SECRET WEAPON #1 – A 'YES I CAN' PHILOSOPHY

Now that I have proven to myself how possible it is to pull together great property development deals, it is amazing to me how daunting this seems to outsiders. I understand that the idea of cranes operating on a neighbourhood site may seem out of reach or intimidating (even though it's my idea of a good time). But the one area that seems to really paralyse people, holding them back from even considering the big goals, is cold hard cash. "I don't have the funds", they say. "How can I ever get into property?"

You need to ask better questions.

You have to be a 'blue-sky' lateral thinker and ask yourself, "What are the tools at my disposal to get in the game with little or no money down? How can I start *now?"*

Even people who *are* cashed up and interested in wealth-building through property tell me the same story. "But Libby, I don't have enough to do something big."

Sure, maybe you can't fund a 54-storey skyscraper in Dubai on your own (and guess what, neither could any property billionaire on his or her first deal). But you *do* have enough for, say, a dilapidated house on a block zoned for dual occupancy (or whatever else is applicable for small investors with a bit of cash). There is always a project to fit a beginner, so start there.

For example, English brothers Nick and Christian Candy are the 30-something developers behind the most expensive property project in British history, One Hyde Park. They have built an empire worth the equivalent of $15 billion and now only develop for the super-rich – that is, when they're not tossing down lobster on their personal mega-yacht. How did they start? With a £6000 loan from their grandmother to buy a flat in grubby, inner-city Earls Court!

Jack Cowin's Beginnings

Jack Cowin appears with steady regularity on the *Business Review Weekly* 'Australian Rich 100' list, has an estimated net worth of $486 million and is someone I am proud to know. He is the Executive Chairman of Competitive Foods Australia and owner of the Hungry Jack's hamburger franchise. He also launched Kentucky Fried Chicken here in Australia in 1969. His company is on track to earn over a billion dollars during the year this book is being published, so it's pretty safe to say he has come a long way. But what I respect enormously about Jack is that he is a self-made man. Even he had to start somewhere.

When I asked him about his beginnings in the game, it was clear that he 'got' real estate from the get-go. "When I was starting off, I didn't really know if people were going to eat hamburgers and Southern fried chicken, but I *did* know that a good piece of property is a great foundation as time goes on. Styles, trends and fashion are unpredictable, but if you own a good piece of real estate and you build on that property, it will always go up in value and be in demand."

Jack needed a way to get into the market. "In those days, borrowing money from banks was nearly impossible; they made it so hard that you had to practically beg. Banks looked at the liquidation value of the real estate – what it would be worth if you defaulted and they had to sell it. Then they would lend you 50 per cent of that liquidation value only. You had to have a lot of cash flow to keep buying property."

He solved his dilemma by coming up with the idea of tapping into the US fast-food movement, borrowing $10,000 each from 30 people so that he didn't have to raise all the capital himself. By the way, those who invested the $10,000 that got Jack on his way in 1969 have an investment worth over $9 million now!

This story illustrates the one ingredient that true go-getters have, even when they are starting with next to nothing. That ingredient is a *can-do attitude* rooted in the determination to find a way – any way – to begin.

The Jack Cowins and Nick and Christian Candys of the world did not start out with silver spoons in their mouths. All they had was the same drive to succeed that you have. Whatever your starting point, the essential first ingredient to property development is knowing in your bones that *you must find a way.* You work with whatever you have to start the climb to wealth as soon as possible.

> **"If you don't believe in yourself who else will? Confidence is everything."**

How I Made My Own Can-Do Attitude Work For Me

When I was in my early twenties and ready to make my way in the world, I discovered a passion for building wealth through property, by diving my nose into self-help, wealth-building books. The only problem was that I didn't have any money.

So I started saving. Once I got to $1000 I was on a roll. By sacrificing everything but necessities (it is amazing how easy it is to blow your whole salary on inessentials) and a steadfast refusal to use credit cards, I established a good savings discipline and kept going until I had $10,000.

I immediately went to see a broker and asked for a loan. The broker told me I was almost there for a full deposit, so I plucked up the courage to ask friends and associates for additional funds. They sensed my drive and discipline, and that I had every intention in the world of paying them back with interest. I threw in a personal loan as well (people usually blow these on cars, boats, toys and furniture). I was ready to move hell and high water to scrape enough together to come back to the broker.

I can almost guarantee you that if you live a simple life of bare minimum spending from your current income, pack your lunches, take the train, lie low and obsessively stick to your purpose for a set period, you will be astonished at how quickly you can save.

This may feel like deprivation, but it's actually the opposite – it's the key to eventual abundance. And this attitude is your first step – the rest of your money will flow from that.

It certainly did for me. From that original deposit, my whole property development career began. As it turned out, I was able to leverage much more than the deposit, because I discovered my next secret weapon – property options.

SECRET WEAPON #2 – PROPERTY OPTIONS

What happens when a developer wants to buy a crumbling old unit block with a garage blocking out its ocean views in order to rebuild something spectacular, but each unit is individually owned?

Or when there are four houses in a row that would make a great land parcel?

What if a developer is interested in a house with great DA potential, but would only want to purchase it with formal council approval?

Sometimes deals only work when you gain either further information or total control. There is no point in committing funds to buy each unit in a killer block if that little old lady in No. 4 won't budge at any price – that renders the other units worthless to you. You may not get DA approval for adding value to a property that looks promising on paper. But what if you could put a property and its big buying costs 'on hold' until you were sure that the deal was going to work and *then* buy?

Well, you can.

An 'option to buy' is the right, but not the obligation, to buy a property at a negotiated price within a set time. The time and price are decided in advance.

If you make an offer and the owner agrees, you put an option on the property to buy yourself some time yet still lock in the deal by paying as little as one dollar. That property is now legally on hold and unavailable to other buyers while you complete your feasibility study, apply for the DA, make offers on neighbouring properties or whatever it is that you want to do with that time.

At the end of the option period, you can make the decision to 'exercise' the option – i.e. go ahead with the purchase on the previously agreed-upon terms – having committed very little funds to obtain the security of full control over the property.

If you decide not to purchase, the owner gets to keep the option fee – bully for them – and you have escaped from an unprofitable purchase with a comparatively minuscule commitment of time and money. This is a fantastic way to secure a property that could skyrocket in value. For example, a property on today's market could be worth about $1.5 million. To increase the property value, you have to make a development application, so you option the property at $1.5 million. The development application requires at least a 12-month option, so for example, you may put down an option fee of either one per cent of the buying price or a flat fee of $10,000 (or even $1, as I have) – very little investment for that kind of value.

The moral of the story? Property options are a spectacular way to get your foot in the door with reduced risk and very little money down.

Options Without a Downpayment

An alternate strategy is to put no money down. In the option agreement, I will add a clause stating that I will lodge the DA within three months of the option period. This shows the owner that I am investing my time and money into the property, and proves that I am actively working to increase its value. I'm not wasting their time by holding them to a 12-month option on the property. This is a great negotiation tool to avoid paying money up front, and it shows the client exactly how I intend to pay the $1.5 million at the end of the option period.

The Best Ways To Profit from Options

Here are some good ways to leverage the use of options.

Option the site, and then sell the option to someone else. You found the site first, and may have optioned it at a certain price. Another developer may still make a profit even by paying you more – and you have made money without laying a brick or doing the DA!

Option the site, do the DA and get it approved. You have added the value by the DA approval process without necessarily even buying the property itself.

Option the site and do a joint venture (discussed in detail below) to get the DA done or the site built. Your joint venture partner needs you because you control the site. You can use their interest in the property by leveraging their money to finance the DA application and/or development and still share in the profits.

Putting an Option in Place

So you've found a great site and completed an initial site analysis that looks feasible. How do you put an option on the property to pin it down? You will need to follow these steps:

- Approach the owner.

- Agree on a value for the site.

- Agree on the date when you will buy the property for the agreed price.

- Agree on an option fee (usually between one and three per cent, though there is no legal requirement).

- Draw up the option contract.

- Prepare the option fee amount.

- Execute the option contract and pay the option fee promptly.

Options Are the Ultimate Leverage Tool

An option is a tiny one to three per cent investment that brings you, the investor, some fantastic advantages:

- You get to **buy time** while you get the DA approved, the financing lined up and your feasibility checklist completed without having to commit the full deposit.

- You **lock in the site** at today's value in case the market value increases before you are ready to buy.

- You **freeze the property,** which legally comes off the market, so you don't have to worry about someone else getting the deal while you complete your due diligence.

This extraordinary tool allows an investor to put down one per cent of the cost and still earn 100 per cent of the profit!

The Best Way to Explain Options to a Property Owner

No one really likes to think that you, as a new buyer, will make more money from their property than they will; it's human nature. So when you tell someone that you are interested in purchasing their property, emphasize that *you* will be the one spending all the money and time working with the council, getting the DA approved and doing the building, and *you* will be the one taking all the risk and investment.

Most people don't think in terms of delayed gratification – even though you, as a good developer, are training yourself to see the great potential benefits ahead. Most property owners will prefer the 'right here, right now' option of taking the money you offer now rather than doing all that work themselves, especially if they have never even thought of property development and don't have a clue what it entails.

Tell the prospective vendor that you would like to pay them a fee now to put a hold on the property instead of purchasing it outright, as you still need to determine whether or not you want to go ahead. Explain that the option fee is theirs to keep no matter what happens, but that they can't sell the property to anyone else while the option is still outstanding. There is no point in explaining the technical details and confusing them with a lot of industry jargon, so just keep it simple and be honest.

There is nothing like handing over a cheque to show people that you are serious, so offer to pay them straight away and lock in the deal. If I can option a good property that can make me great profit, I don't quibble over a few thousand dollars and am happy to pay fair market value as long as there is profit to be made over the long haul.

Putting Options into Practice in Real Life

After raising a deposit and finding my first house, I learned all about zoning at council. The informative people there tipped me off and suggested that rather than simply building two townhouses on the site I had just bought, I should try to buy the neighbouring property and build even more, thus maximising the return on my investment.

Council gave me two crucial documents to read: the *DCP Development Control Planning Guide*, which was about 300 pages long, and the *LEP Land and Environment Planning Guide*. I studied them cover to cover as part of my education as a property developer. I'll reiterate that these guides are the 'bibles' for any designated council area, allowing you to master the parameters of local development and to know what you should go out and option.

My research told me that I would indeed optimise the value of the land I already owned if I bought more of it and sought permission to build nine townhouses. All well and good, but I didn't have the cash on hand to purchase the extra land next door.

I was a young kid, but I was still smart enough to know what I *didn't* know, so I started picking the brains of developers working in the area to understand the best way forward (a willingness to talk to strangers is mission critical in the property game). Once I knew there was a way to greatly increase the property value and my own profit, I knew I had to go for it. See what I mean about having a can-do attitude? This led me right to the 'options' step.

These experienced developers explained options to me, telling me how they would hold many properties this way, gaining control over them while they consulted architects, did their pricing, reviewed council regulations and submitted their proposals. When they told me they didn't even need to purchase the property, it blew my mind. I could take a raw site and get paid for just putting the deal together? Why wasn't everyone doing this? Suddenly I saw how I could get in the game on a much bigger scale.

After some back-and-forth negotiations, I optioned the two houses next door to my original purchase and completed a development application for nine townhouses, investing a total of $4300 in option fees and $22,000 in DA costs. I obtained these funds quickly through a personal loan and a credit card, and when I on-sold the nine-townhouse, pre-approved package I made a whopping profit of $170,000, all leveraged from my original small deposit and a few subsequent expenses! Of course, I would always recommend using seed money instead of credit cards as you start gaining wealth, but these were my first baby steps.

I was on a roll from that very first deal, knocking on doors wherever I spotted a potential development site. I optioned a row of four houses with the potential for 30 units in that space, then on-sold it to developers who paid me well for this new added value – *even though I never owned the original property in the first place.* With the money I was making, I bought houses I thought would be re-zoned in the short term (after extensive research and study). One home that I bought for $335,000 was re-zoned as a high-rise designation, so I re-sold it for more than $1 million to developers less than a year later.

Property options buy you time and, if you are starting out, a way into property investment without needing to have the cash upfront.

SECRET WEAPON #3 – JOINT VENTURES

An old maxim says that it's better to have 50 per cent of something than 100 per cent of nothing. You may come across a deal that is out of your reach because you can only fund a portion of it, or even none of it! But if a deal is profitable, someone somewhere will be interested in sharing the load – and the profit – with you by becoming your co-investor.

A joint venture ('JV') is a legal entity formed as a short-term partnership with another party or parties so that you can officially act and invest as a team. Obviously each party adds a value proposition to the deal. The simplest example would be a case in which two parties each invest 50 per cent of the cost, then take 50 per cent of the profit.

While many JVs simply unite people who are investing certain percentages of the necessary funds, sometimes the assets one party brings to a JV are quite different from those of the other party or parties. Money can be invested, but so can time, contacts, skill and specific knowledge. The profits are split among the parties in whatever ratio has been determined *before* finalising the deal.

There are no rules about what a JV must be – it is limited only by your imagination. Together, you and your JV partners can do deals that you couldn't or wouldn't do alone.

JVs with No Money Down

So how do you do a JV if you have no money to bring to the table at all? Here's one example to get you thinking.

A development application can cost anything from $20,000 to $300,000, depending on what you're developing (two townhouses, say, vs a 30-unit block). If you don't have this money, you simply need to find a partner who does.

But that doesn't mean you have nothing to bring to the table! You can do the due diligence, verify the site, location and profit margin, and option a good property. You can then partner with a professional developer, get them to do the DA and pay all the costs, and then split the profits in half. Essentially, you have put together a deal with no money down and partnered with an expert who is willing to take on the associated costs. If the DA doesn't go through, then the loss will fall on the developer at no cost to you!

A 'No Money Down' JV in Real Life

A perfect example of how pivotal JVs can be to building wealth is the one that 'brought me back from the dead' after I lost all the original wealth I'd created in property development. I had made the classic rookie mistake of not preparing for a rainy day or property downturn. As I talked about at the beginning of this book, I left myself exposed and cash-poor, which forced me to liquidate at the worst possible time. And yes, I'd bought into the image trap and purchased 'big toys' on top of everything. D'oh!

So I started an online business and worked at it for a few years to get my cash flow up again and my basic bills paid. But I missed property development and knew it was time to get back to my first love. I was humble enough to start from scratch, but had enough belief in my skills, based on my prior success, to go out and find some great deals.

I approached the developers with whom I had developed a personal affinity, who had seen what I had achieved in my early years and still believed in me. I proposed that I go out and find deals, do all the grunt work and feasibility studies, then present them with the best of the best – feasible deals with an attractive profit margin of 15 to 30 per cent. They would fund the deals, but I would do all the initial and subsequent work to make them come to life and increase the property values. They had nothing to lose and everything to gain – so this is how I started building my wealth again, one brick at a time utilising my property development education.

This is what one of our typical JVs looked like. I contributed 100 per cent of the time to search for the right deal, using my skill to recognise one when I saw it and running the feasibility study on it. Once we agreed to purchase the property, my partner contributed 100 per cent of the investment funds, while I did all the work to manage the project. When done, we each got 50 per cent of the profits.

This was a win-win situation for all of us. My partners made a good return with zero effort, while remaining free to run their own businesses without interruption. And I started to rebuild my portfolio and get money back in my coffers with no money down – the perfect solution for someone with skill and more time than money.

After the first deal went through, in which we added value to a block of units, my investors were encouraged to roll the original investment plus all of their profits into the next deal. I ended up with money in the bank and two investment units to hold. I was on my way again!

JVs can also be a great vehicle for you to start your experience in property development. You find and structure the deals, and others put up the cash in return for a guaranteed return or a percentage of whatever the profits are.

"Develop property for profit."

Vendor-Related JVs

Sometimes a property owner has a site that is ripe for development but needs an experienced property developer to assist. In such cases the owner and developer join in what is known as a 'vendor-related' JV. What that means for you is that even if you don't own the land yourself, you can still get a fair price and percentage of the profits by helping someone else develop theirs.

The acting developer on any JV needs access to the equity from his or her JV partners to secure the construction loan for work done on the property. If you become the acting developer, this means the owner(s) must sign over equity to you. You will also need exclusive access to the property itself for the duration of the due diligence period. This will allow you to complete your feasibility study, get the DA approved, and explore the property with the technicians, surveyors and consultants you engage for the project.

Advantages of JVs

There are many advantages to doing a joint venture, including the following:

- **Strength in numbers.** The group as a whole becomes greater than the sum of its parts; each person contributes a missing piece of the jigsaw. Joining forces puts a better deal within reach of people who would not otherwise be able to participate.

- **Safety in numbers.** Because you are spreading the investment among several parties, the risk for each individual is lowered.

- **Increased financial rating.** Banks lend money based on experience. Initial involvement through a JV can help you build a positive portfolio that banks will look upon favourably in the future.

- **Decreased learning curve.** You can join forces with people who have more money and experience than you do and learn from them as you go through each stage.

- **No money down.** You can exchange a finder's fee and project management time into real property equity by the end of the project. You can still get in the game!

The Best Way to Create a Solid JV

Here is how to ensure you create a watertight joint venture that will net you and your partner(s) a nice profit.

No matter who invests the capital, it should be deposited into a trust set up specifically for the JV. This capital is managed by a trustee, and all revenue flows back into the trust. This keeps everything legal, aboveboard and monitored by an external authority. No access is granted to the revenue until all investors have been paid according to the terms of the JV.

Make the trust about just one project, and include the specific address of the property involved.

Good ethics in all aspects of the JV are paramount. You can't put a dollar value on your reputation. If investors can't trust you, they won't let you use their money!

Never pay for the land that your JV is developing upfront – pay for it out of the profits.

Don't be greedy! Be fair and keep a win-win viewpoint in mind so that everyone is motivated and will want to work with you again.

Make the JV agreement a legally binding document signed by witnesses. In it, list all of the following:

- Role of the venture

- Roles of each person involved

- Capital contributions to be made

- Shares of ownership

- Management of the venture

- Duration of the venture, including both best-case and worst-case scenarios (making sure the worst-case scenario really is, because the investors will be annoyed if the project is overdue past these pre-set expectations)

- Loan guarantors (financially responsible party or parties in the event someone defaults on the loan)

- Outline of how any disputes will be handled (e.g. describe the dispute resolution process and list the solicitor to be used). Typically in business you want to go through arbitration as opposed to legal proceedings

- Outline of how shareholders may cash out if they decide to leave the project.

*Ensure you consult a professional to set up the right structure for you and your specific deal.

Once you have mastered the art of launching property deals with plenty to offer, even from very humble financial beginnings, you will be more than ready to raise the finance for future deals yourself.

"It's better to have 50 per cent of something than 100 per cent of nothing."

To access your free webinar training now, simply go to:

www.LibbyLombardo.com/bonus

LEVERAGEACADEMY

CHAPTER EIGHT:
Show Me the Money —
Financing Your Deal

" *Money is just an idea backed by confidence.* "

CHAPTER EIGHT: SHOW ME THE MONEY – FINANCING YOUR DEAL

A time will come when you have the track record and assets to raise your own funds – or maybe you are already cashed up or can service a loan, and you want to be the one controlling the finances. In either case, cash flow and profits are things all developers learn to work with. Being informed and empowered around money is one of the great attitude shifts that developing property will bring you.

ASK THE EXPERTS

I believe in delegating to specialists. Just as I am happy to offer my development skills to cashed-up clients who have neither the time nor the inclination to develop property yet still want to avail themselves of that 20 per cent profit, I am happy to bow to the superior knowledge of accountants, mortgage brokers and lawyers when it comes to the fine points of finance and law.

First and foremost, finance rules change, so it is not crucial that you know everything about financing. Even if you skip the rest of this chapter, other sources will help you through these basics. What *is* important is knowing where to look for finance information and financial advisors whom you can trust. Property investors use experts in many areas throughout a project, to help them understand structure, loan and tax issues. Here's where you'll need some expert help.

Loan matching. A mortgage broker knows all the pre-existing conditions from bank to bank and has established relationships with their lenders. A broker can help match your project with the right commercial or residential lender and loan product, acting as a professional liaison between you and the bank. The great news is that their services don't cost a thing as their commission comes straight out of your interest payment to the bank.

Pre-construction. This includes planning costs, budgeting, project auditing and the holding costs of the interest on borrowed money.

Construction. You need to constantly assess the state of the construction. Are you on budget? How much have you eaten into your contingency allowance at each stage?

Post-construction. This is your final accounting status. Every dollar has to be accounted for in your balance sheet.

Tax depreciation. There are depreciation schedules for selling the property; you'll want to optimise your tax breaks here.

Approximate price calculations. You should budget for appropriate prices throughout the project. One rule of thumb, for example, is that building costs per square metre might be $1500 to $1600 for a nice site or $3000 to $3500 for an upmarket site (depending on what you are building).

APPLYING FOR FINANCING

Before getting too invested in any project, you'll need to determine how best to finance your deal. Some of the popular options are:

Vendor financing. Rather than purchasing the property outright, either with your own funds or those borrowed from the bank, you pay a partial amount to the vendor who retains title on the property until you finish your final repayments and pay out the balance of what you owe. It's like a lay-by, except you access the asset before final purchase.

Mezzanine financing. This occurs when various lenders lend out different portions of the total funds at varying rates of interest. The lower the interest the lender charges, the higher they are in the hierarchy of lenders. If anything goes wrong, they are first in line for liquidation. The less risk-averse lenders who charge the highest amount of interest are last in line if the project fails. Typically set at around 12 to 22 per cent these days, interest rates like this are still reasonable for smaller portions of your deal – they get it across the line and give you access to bigger profits later. For example, in a $2 million deal, if a bank will lend you around $1 million, then mezzanine financing could bridge the gap for you.

Venture capital. Developers can structure deals with venture capitalists, who provide seed money for potentially profitable projects or companies in their early stages. The profit margin usually has to be around 23 to 25 per cent for a venture capitalist to get involved, and he or she will typically take around 25 per cent of the profits. But again, 75 per cent of something is better than 100 per cent of nothing.

Syndicate. A syndicate is a group of investors who pool their money to buy a property and share in the profit so that everyone wins. You formally create a legal vehicle such as a trust or company to form the syndicate, which will be public or private depending on who your investors are and what everyone wants out of the deal.

The Golden Rule

When applying to a bank or investor for money, the golden rule is to be professional in every respect, from correspondence to dress. Look like you know what you are doing and you are more likely to walk away with the loan you want. *Remember that money is just an idea backed by confidence.* Your bank application should include:

- Your final, detailed feasibility study for the bank's independent verification

- Comparable sales figures from RPData.com

- The development application itself and any special conditions

- A picture or artist's impression of the property

- Confirmation from real estate agents on their recent sales in the area

- A site summary

- Market research

- A projected sales schedule outlining: (a) when you will start selling; (b) how many units you will sell per month; and (c) which agent you will use.

"Dream, believe, create, achieve."

Further Research

I will not go into the minutiae of finance structures and strategies available to you, as you will need to consult with specialists and that is not the role of this book. But here is a brief outline of items you should be aware of.

Certificate of Title

The government tracks everything that happens with a particular property, from actual ownership to any 'financial incumbencies' (e.g. mortgages) on it, using its certificate of title. And the party that provided the finance has claim to that property as security if the lender defaults on the loan repayments.

If a property with multiple mortgages is sold, the payment is applied according to a hierarchy. For example, on a property with three outstanding mortgages, the first mortgagee has first right to repayment; the second mortgagee comes next and so on. Clearly, the further down the hierarchy a mortgagee is, the less security there is – and therefore, the smaller the likelihood of repayment in case of default.

Trusts

As a budding property developer, you should familiarise yourself with this financial structure that holds funds in another name, and under a variety of legal umbrellas. Traditionally, trusts offer asset protection, flexibility in funding distributing and clear definitions of estate planning and the passing on of assets. The top five per cent of income earners in Australia have set up the vast majority of its trusts; financially successful people use them as a common tool to protect and manage their earnings. You can and should join them.

There are many types of trusts, but for developers, the unit trust is one of the most important. A unit trust is a public trading trust formed by a syndicate of 50 or more investors. For those who want to develop units for resale or holding, this can be a very viable alternative to creating a private company.

A unit trust has several advantages:

- A deed determines who owns what percentage of the property. The unit holders' interests in the assets and income are clearly defined.

- Units can be easily transferred or redeemed.

- Unit holders are governed by a unit trust deed that can be tailored for specific needs.

- Trusts involve less regulation than companies.

- Trusts are easier to wind up.

Other types of trusts include discretionary trusts, hybrid trusts, individual trusts and company trusts, all of which may need to be considered depending on your goals. Does this make your head hurt? Me too. So consult your financial consultant and let him or her do the head-spinning for you.

Goods and Services Tax

You need to be aware of the concessions available for potential property buyers through the Goods and Services Tax ('GST') for purchasers of 'new' residential, commercial or industrial property. You can claim this back off your taxes.

Negative and Positive Gearing

'Negative gearing' refers to the initial loss in the early stages of property investment due to the high level of debt involved in the purchase, in which the rental income on the property is less than the interest on the loan, depreciation and holding costs (e.g. the rental agency commission). These losses can be an advantage when offset against your personal income tax if they have the means to keep 'topping up' this monthly expense out of their own pocket. This is why accountants love negative gearing. You pay less tax elsewhere while the capital worth of your property rises.

Other investors seek out 'positive gearing', in which the rental income exceeds the costs right from the start. They figure, "If I am paying more tax, then I may as well be making more money, too". Investors also sometimes do this when they do not have the cash flow to fill any gaps between their income and expenses every month. Positive gearing means they are not exposed to the risk of defaulting on payments. The property simply pays for itself – and then some.

Gearing is a matter of choice in how you structure a property purchase. High-income investors can carry a negative gearing burden, and it may reduce their tax. I know other people whose focus is retiring early with a passive income and want the positive cash flow to start rolling in immediately. You should sit down with your accountant and work out which strategy is for you, as this will affect the kind of property that you will invest in.

Interest-Only Loans

Paying interest-only on your loan can free up excess cash flow *if you put that cash to good use.* If you blow that savings on 'toys', then of course it would be better to use it to slowly reduce the principal amount as well. But used wisely, it frees up money to leave in a mortgage offset account until you save enough for a deposit on your next property, giving you access to *new* rental income or sales profits.

THE MAGIC THRESHOLD

Your overall goal is to reach that 'magic threshold' where your first debt is reduced enough to convince the bank to lend you funds for your next property or site. There are tools to help you reach this threshold more quickly.

Capital Gain. This option is for those who are holding, not selling, their properties. As each investment starts to climb in worth, you can borrow against this new equity to raise the deposit for the next property.

Deposit Bonds. If you are selling and using the proceeds of one deal to finance the next, you can buy a deposit bond from a financial institution, which guarantees the deposit amount until your own funds are freed up from your sale. This means you can act on a great deal before you have settled on the last one.

Deferred Settlement. This helps you buy time to get your financing together. You pin down the property or site with a deposit, but are granted a much longer time than the standard six weeks to settle in full.

THE LIBBY LOMBARDO FINANCIAL PHILOSOPHY IN A NUTSHELL

Seek Expert Advice

You can master property development, but you really don't have to master accounting and tax law. You are better off tapping into someone else's expertise in this regard.

Be Visionary, not Risky

Think big, but never gamble. Have your JV partners, feasibility studies, lending guarantees and whatever else helps you get that deal over the line in place *before* you commit and become financially liable.

Maximise Your Dollar

Let your money work for you so that you can retire young and wealthy. If the money you have invested in a completed development would be better off in a second deal, sell and liquidate it. If the potential capital gain is too great, then hold onto the property, rent it out and borrow against it. Is a boom about to hit in another area because of a new highway or hospital? Do your research.

Don't coast – always make sure that your precious funds are in the absolute best place to grow for you so that you don't just work hard, you work *smart.* One day your growing portfolio will do *all* the work.

"Turn the invisible into the visible."

CHAPTER NINE:
The Buy and Negotiations

" In real estate, the buy is the factor that makes or breaks a deal from the get-go. "

CHAPTER NINE: THE BUY AND NEGOTIATIONS

So you've mastered the next hot suburb, raised your funds, found the right JV partner (or decided to go solo) and are now ready to stroll on court and hit one over the net.

Here is where rookies often think, "I'm raring to go, so I'll grab whatever is out there and worry about selling for a profit later, post-development". But any property guru will tell you that *all the advantages of the deal have to be built in upfront.* Movie directors usually say that 90 per cent of their job is done with the casting, long before the first day of shooting; the project stands or falls on these initial choices. Well, in real estate, the buy is the factor that makes or breaks a deal from the get-go.

That's why you learn as much as you can and minimise your risks. The property you're working with has to be sellable because in the end, that's the only reason you're developing it. Potential profit margins will be pointless if your property is in a bad location or impossible if you pay too much going in.

After almost twenty years in the business, I can safely say that this is one of the most crucial elements of the trade. **It all starts with 'the get'!** You must be strategic about choosing a site bursting with profit potential because property developers are all about adding value. The better the initial purchase, the easier it will be to get the project down the administrative pipeline and move your finished product.

So here is my criteria for getting that great buy.

THE RIGHT LOCATION

If you have seriously studied Chapter Three on finding the right site and done your follow-up research, you are searching for a good location where future buyers or tenants will want to live.

Location drives absolutely everything in the real estate game. No matter how attractive a piece of property is, if you can't get to it easily or get to anywhere of interest from it, no one will want to buy or rent it. This means proximity to one, but preferably more, of the following:

- Schools

- Hospitals

- Universities and colleges

- Transportation

- Shopping strips/centres

- Beach

- The central business district

- A secondary, satellite central business district.

The area you have selected may be family-friendly, with great playgrounds and an aquatic centre; the neighbouring suburb may have just shot up and priced out those who will now flow into your choice of a new hot spot, creating new demand.

Your selection may be based on capital growth in the area, which exceeds the national average, showing strong demand year in and year out. Sometimes the more glamorous suburbs are on a downturn or are flat lining while the 'ugly duckling' suburbs are experiencing growth. It's all in the research!

Regardless of the details, by the time you are ready to buy, you have strategically chosen a solid investment in an area with excellent growth prospects.

THE RIGHT PROPERTY

Now you are looking at the interesting properties for sale in your area or areas of choice. Naturally you have done your feasibility study from Chapter Four and weeded out the deal-breakers – bushfire zones, asbestos material, the neighbour with 60 television sets on the front lawn or a high-voltage substation next door.

You have identified a good site – a large block that you can subdivide, an opportunity to provide the neighbourhood with a commercial entity it desperately needs, rear access or the right zoning to build higher-density housing. Over the years, you will probably develop a preference. In my case, I usually look for corner properties that are in prime locations, near the main action.

THE RIGHT DEAL

Make sure the deal you're contemplating works *today*. You want the feasibility study to show that a profit is there straight away when you buy a property. *Do not* fall into the trap of airy-fairy rationales about future profits ("There is no profit in it now, but the area will go up in value while I build", "If I wait long enough someone will pay me more", "I'll get lucky" or "It always works out in the end"). Property development is not about crossing fingers or leaping off cliffs; it's about in-the-bag numbers that prove you can make a profit *now*. Any capital gains you make are just a bonus, so don't count on them.

Don't do 'maybes' either ("We *may* make more money if we put in a pool", "The other people in the block *may* move out", or "I *may* be able to buy the roof rights"). It will take years longer to recoup profit this way.

I built Leverage Property with on-paper profits based on the solid proof of 'now' prices and 'now' possibilities. You want to know that if you sold tomorrow, you'd still be ahead. That way you can rest easy and be happy with the return on your investment as soon as you buy.

THE RIGHT PRICE

It all begins with your buy-in cost!

This point is key. While I always award 10 points out of 10 for enthusiasm and creativity (the more deals you bring to the table, the more you are starting to think like a property developer), one of the most common mistakes I see new developers make is creating a property package with no promising start-off price.

There are many reasons why this can happen. The site may have been picked over by competitors in the open marketplace. Perhaps there are no mitigating factors to make it a bargain. Or maybe the sub-par negotiation skills of the inexperienced, overemotional investor guarantee that he or she will never flush out the vendor's lowest price.

My strategy? **Buy low.**

Pretty obvious, right? You'd think so. But many new developers forget that a dollar saved buying in is just as valuable as a dollar gained selling out. They get so caught up in nabbing the deal that they will even pay a premium to beat the next guy.

Anyone can buy at top dollar, but a Leverage Property developer always remembers my rule: **Make money as soon as you buy**.

Buying sites for top dollar will dramatically shrink your future profit margins. It may take you some years just to recoup what you lost from paying too much initially. That in turn creates 'opportunity cost' – profits you could have rolled into future developments are tied up while you wait for your asset to catch up with the market.

But the 'get' of buying a bargain at the best possible price, even at under-market value, puts money in the bank right at the outset. You are ahead before you have even built or added any value. This first step is the foundation for your future profits – more solid than any concrete, and paying off long before you drill your first hole.

This advice bears repeating – a dollar saved buying in is going to be worth just as much as a dollar made selling out!

Why pay market price or more when there are so many ways to avoid it?

"You don't know what you don't know till you know it." – Richard Pratt

MY TOOLS FOR BUYING LOW

The main idea here is to look for someone who wants to sell even more than you want to buy. We call this a 'motivated vendor' – someone who is very pressed to sell, perhaps to the point where they will still come out ahead if they accept your low offer. There are a variety of reasons why people are willing to offload property at a lower-than-market price.

Finance

The owner may be structuring a deal and has already committed money from this site to the next one. If the sale has taken longer than anticipated, it will be more costly to renege on the next deal than to reduce the profits on this one – which turns out to be your good fortune. Timing is a huge motivator for people to sell low.

Bankruptcy

When an owner fails to pay creditors, they can officially declare the owner bankrupt. A professional liquidator takes control of the owner's assets, converting them into whatever cash they can to cover part or all of the debt. The liquidator is not interested in sitting on a property to wait out a great price – it just wants to move it fast so that impatient creditors can start getting paid.

Mortgage Sales and Possession

When the owner's mortgage payments are too far in arrears (unpaid), the lender can repossess the property and take over power of sale. All the bank wants is to get its loan amount back – any extra goes to the owner, but the owner has little say in the matter. Although laws do prevent fire sales, the buyer of such a property is still not dealing with a picky owner who is in control.

DA Approval Time Period

If an owner has run out of time to get the construction or finance together before the DA on a property expires (at which point its value will drop sharply), the owner is likely to be motivated to sell quickly and low. If you, on the other hand, are ready to develop in time, then you can take this sinking asset and capitalise on its full potential while paying only its 'sinking value' price.

Emotional Reasons

Some owners just want out for emotional, not logical, reasons, be it a divorce, family feud or acrimony between business partners who want to split ways as soon as possible. If you can give them their wish by offering them a quick way out, the owner(s) may take you up on your lowball offer.

Earlier Bad Buyers

Inexperienced or 'mum and dad' developers may have rushed into buying a site without seeing it purely as a business deal. Now that they have done the DA their figures don't stack up or their funding has fallen through. You are willing to take it off their hands for far less – what they should have paid in the first place.

Always ask the agent, "Why are they selling?" If a property owner is holding out for the top price and doesn't care if they sell any time soon, generally speaking you should move on and look for an opportunity where the seller is motivated to sell. On the other hand, the agent's answer may indicate a motivated vendor. Either way, the more you know, the better.

Sales by Owner

Look in the newspaper for advertisements from people who are trying to sell property themselves. Drive around and look for 'For Sale by Owner' signs. These property owners normally want to sell in a hurry and want to save on the approximately 2 to 2.5 per cent agency fees. You can deal directly with them yourself, taking into account all the money they are saving on an agent – maybe even splitting the savings (which could be as high as $15,000 or more) down the middle and taking $7500 off the asking price.

I like private sales and often deal with owners. You don't have the real estate agent trying to skilfully haggle with you for the best price, or use your bid to drive a competitor up. Also, agents act as buffers, whereas private sellers who are not in the real estate business may be less willing to constantly negotiate or have strangers tramping through their property.

When you are interested in a property that is selling through an agent, you can safely assume that the listed sales price is meant to reflect a little negotiating room, so automatically knock 10 per cent off to determine what the sellers' optimum expectations are.

Solve People's Problems

When you are flexible and work with the owner, you become the buyer who can get them what they want or need – which could mean a compromise on price. Does the owner want a long settlement? A short settlement? To stay on and rent for six months? A cherry on top? If it works within your feasibility parameters, consider their need as a bargaining point and leverage it into a discount.

I have made offers to settle in two weeks with no cooling-off period to get people out of trouble; I got those properties at great prices and saved myself thousands of dollars. The sky is the limit when dreaming up a good deal! But don't depend on the owner for this – think outside the box and create some problem-solving ideas that will work for both parties and put you ahead of your competitors.

Market Timing

At times property values are booming and everyone is jumping into the game, naturally wanting to believe that the increases will never end. Think of the late 1990s and early 2000s, when property values kept going up and up. People assumed that this skyrocketing growth was long-term and hopped on the gravy train at any price, right at the height of the market.

This is often when smart property investors lay low and stay out of the frenzy. They save their funds for when the correction hits, the over-borrowing stops, values are dropping and everyone else is desperately trying to get out of the market. The whole market has moved in the buyer's favour, and this is sometimes well worth the wait.

Auctions

I usually prefer buying property that is listed for immediate sale. It's much less stressful than buying at auction – with auctions, buyers have to wait for the auction date, the outcome is unknown and the sales price reflects whatever the market offers that day. If the property is for sale, or you are approaching a private owner, you can start negotiating straight away (see the section on negotiation).

However, many sites and houses are offered for sale by auction, where potential buyers bid against each other in real time and prices can rise in increments of thousands, sometimes tens of thousands (though this tendency can lessen as lower bidders fall away and the bidding slows down, getting closer to the final price).

Vendors choose auctions in the hope that at least two emotional buyers will start a bidding frenzy driven by the desire for the property and fear of losing it; many buyers overpay under the stress and pressure of a live auction. In the heat of the moment, they reach prices they would never have offered in the relative calm of their homes or offices.

Buying at auction can be a good way to pick up a bargain if you don't have any bullish competitors counter-bidding, if people don't show up for personal reasons – sometimes even just because of bad weather. The lack of counter-interest (which an agent would normally conceal on a sale property) is thus exposed for all to see.

Many developers have snapped up bargains because they showed up at the right auction when other interest was slow or low-priced. To do this, you have to be prepared to go to many auctions that exceed your price as well. Auctions have unknown outcomes, so you have to cast the net wide.

Here are some tips for keeping a cool head at property auctions.

Never get carried away with the emotion of the auction itself. Auctions are fast-paced and very exciting; people get competitive and carried away with winning 'their' particular property at any cost. If you have never been to a real estate auction, I suggest you visit one without any intention to bid or buy anything so that you can attune yourself to the excitement.

Set yourself a price limit and stick to it. Remember your feasibility and be guided only by that maximum price. If the bidding goes one cent over your price, you're out. Sit back and enjoy the show while someone else overpays.

Bid Late. An auction is like a game of poker; only in this case you can see everyone's hand before you place a bet. Don't even place a bid until you have seen what everyone else is doing. Lull them into thinking that they are the only players. Then, if the bidding is still in your price range, put your first bid in at the auctioneer's 'going twice' (when the property is about to be sold to the highest bidder). Even though you may be right at the end of your tether price-wise, it looks to other buyers like you are only just beginning to bid, and this may scare them off.

If it doesn't sell. Many sellers at auction have a reserve price, which is the absolute lowest price at which they will consider selling the item or property. The bidders cannot see the reserve price while bidding, but they will know if it is met, because the auctioneer will announce that it is now officially "on the market and will be sold".

If the bidding doesn't reach the reserve price, try negotiating with the seller afterward. The property wouldn't be at auction in the first place if the owner wasn't very keen to sell it quickly, and auctions are expensive to run. They may let it go for under the reserve price afterwards, just to get the property sold on the day.

NEGOTIATION

Negotiating is an art form, and I have honed my skills over many handshakes with all kinds of different people. That is the fun of property development – you never know what combination of people will be brought together to swap property and cash assets, possibly never to meet again.

Here are some tips that help demystify the negotiation process and even make it enjoyable.

Negotiating is about relationship-building first and foremost. As a prospective buyer keen to acquire a site, you need to understand the owner – who they are, what they do, what their problems are, why they are selling and solve their problems. People will sell to you because they like you. Rather than act like a hard-headed businessperson, understand your vendor and gently guide them in the direction you'd like.

Make **low** *bidding personal.* It's best to give a potential vendor a reason why you can only go so high. "We were thinking low 700s, but may be able to stretch ourselves to pay 750K. That's all we can borrow." Something like this is more appealing than an arrogant, combative approach that is all about getting them to come down in price so you can make more money.

Get them to name the price first. If the seller is the first person in the negotiation to name a price, you will know where he or she stands and work from there. When you offer a price first you may unwittingly overshoot and start higher than their initial number. There is no advantage in exposing your price range first – far better to identify what the seller is thinking before you reveal your hand. A good departure point is, "What would you be happy with?" This way, when you counter-offer with a lower price that is still in the ballpark, you are in their 'happy' area.

Always underplay. After hearing that first number (or seeing the asking price), always offer less than that number. If you have nothing to start with, you have nothing to lose. Very rarely will a seller walk away from the negotiating table after your first offer, so offer lower than the asking price. Just be careful not to lowball to such a degree that you compromise your rapport – sellers are often emotionally attached to a property, and you don't want to insult them.

Always do the negative takeaway. Rather than betraying your neediness for their fantastic site (even if it is the find of the century), let them get in touch with their neediness by showing them how easily you could slip through their fingers. Be casual and noncommittal; indicate that they would be lucky to hold your interest. "Sure thing, talk to your husband. I'm not in a hurry and I know there is a fair bit for sale here." Never reveal desperation or desire. Make it clear that you are willing to walk away.

Negotiate with all parties present. If you are negotiating with owners, make sure that the relevant parties are present so that all your hard work won't evaporate when it is passed on secondhand. If a couple is selling, then ensure that both the partners are present to cut out the extra step in the decision-making process. This way they can consult with each other and support each other, and you can seize the moment if you verbally strike a deal.

In my experience, it's mostly the women who make the final decision. Traditionally, women reign over the domestic realm; most husbands are far more eager to buy or sell once they know their wife is happy about the transaction. Even when the man acts like he's in charge, he usually confers with his wife. If she is excited and saying, "Honey, I really want to take $750K and sell", he'll do it. *Talk to him but make her happy.* The same goes for selling. Women get emotional about kitchens and bathrooms and will pay that extra $50 thousand because they are 'in love' with the property.

Control the conversation. A great negotiator deftly leads the conversation and controls the communication without ever making it obvious. The seating arrangement is important. Sit between the couple, one person to your left and one to your right, rather than separately on one side, which subtly reinforces an 'us against them' mentality. The situation should read instead that you are all together, chatting amicably about a win/win deal, and you'd all like to walk away happy. If you sit in the middle, you have the authority in the situation and can control it.

Inevitably, people go off track and bring in irrelevant stories – when this happens, be friendly, acknowledge them and then bring things back to the matter at hand.

I never take a cup of tea or piece of cake upfront in a meeting, as this creates a subtle psychological shift in your host: now you owe them something. (You can tell how tight or giving people are when they offer you a drink. Warm tap water sloshed into a chipped mug says something very different from water served in a chilled glass with a lemon garnish). I suggest you don't impose on people's generosity (or lack thereof) until the end of the meeting when you have the deal. Then the tea and biscuits become a celebration.

One person talks. There are times to be a great team player, and times to be a lone wolf. In property development, it helps to do both well. If another party is adding finance or other specialised expertise to a deal and wants to be there when you make a direct offer to an owner, or even if your personal assistant is along for the ride to learn about the business, you don't need more noise.

I find that other people wrestle control away from the conversation I am trying to build. At best, their opinion just adds clutter and slows the process down with extra small talk. At worst, a companion's chatter will add too much pressure to your pitch, contradict something you have said earlier or even sabotage a deal. I have no idea what they will blurt out next or if it will do more harm than good.

What if your companion is better and more experienced than you? Great – let them handle things for the first few deals, and stay quiet yourself. Let only one negotiator take the stage; don't let a group dilute the laser-beam focus of one voice and one vision. One person getting you over the line is an opportunity; two people feels more like pressure.

Seal the Deal. The salesman's number-one rule is 'always be closing the deal'. If you have done your feasibility, and the owner has nominated a number that is within negotiating room of it, you should aim to close the deal right there and then. You don't want to lose momentum when the right number is agreed upon, so verbally seal the deal and reconfirm the deal.

You are the one who must drive this deal home. When a number that works brilliantly with your feasibility is close enough to their price, indicate that you're ready to sign. Nail a price right there and then and don't be too attached to the mental victory or lose a deal over a thousand dollars. Then, offer *them* the congratulations and handshakes. General happiness gives the appearance of a great deal for everyone.

> **"Always listen to a proposition first, you can always so no after."**

Control the outcome with body language. **People feel reassured when you take control. You give your vendors the pen, tell them who to make it out to** and **reassure them that you are putting the deposit or option fee in their bank account that afternoon if they'd like**. When asking them a question, nod 'yes' or shake your head 'no' as you are asking them to nudge the answer your way. ("You don't have any more questions, do you?" as you subtly shake your head no, for example. Or "You would like to get a really good property developer to develop this land so you can sell for a bit of profit, wouldn't you?" as you are nodding yes.) Body language connects directly with the powerful subconscious.

As a property developer, when you buy, you just have to be better than the people looking. And you *will* get better, all the time.

> *"All that we are is the result of what we have thought. The mind is everything. What we think, we become." -* **Buddha**

LIBBY'S LAST WORD

I am a firm believer in education and mentorship as you head out into the real world – on whatever journey that may be.

I have had and continue to have mentors in all aspects of my life. Just as I sought mentorship for help with this book, I suggest you seek someone to champion your journey.

You have come to the end of this book, and now you begin your own property development journey.

Continue to read books, attend seminars and more importantly, get out into the real world, research and take action. Start studying an area, look on the internet, go to auctions and open inspections – become an area expert. Start to build a team around you by asking for referrals to accountants, great real estate agents, builders, draftsman and town planners.

What I have shared with you in this book is only the start of everything you will need to know to do real deals.

I look forward to helping you further and connecting at one of my seminars or online at LibbyLombardo.com, where I share tips and updates in property development.

I wish you every success,

Libby Lombardo

ABOUT LIBBY LOMBARDO

As founder of Leverage Property, Libby Lombardo has traded, sold and developed millions of dollars worth of property. She didn't go from being a high-school dropout to sampling life on a Learjet without a passion for being proactive and making extraordinary things happen! As head of the Leverage Property team, Libby is only too happy to share her incredible journey thus far – and passionate about taking her members along for the ride to great wealth ahead.

You can find out more at www.LibbyLombardo.com.

WOULD YOU LIKE TO PUT YOUR OWN DEVELOPMENT DEAL TOGETHER?

Learning to find a development site is not that hard if you understand all the steps!

I have helped family, friends and many clients successfully put development deals together, if your interested to know more send me an email: deals@libbylombardo.com.au

OR

DO YOU HAVE A DEVELOPMENT SITE BUT YOU NEED HELP DEVELOPING IT?

Many people are already sitting on a development opportunity, It could be your own home, an investment property or someone you know?

I have helped many people turn their existing property into it's full development potential and helped families build great wealth! Send me an email we would love to see if we can help you?

deals@libbylombardo.com.au

LIBBYLOMBARDO
PROPERTY DEVELOPER. SPEAKER. AUTHOR.

LIBBY'S RECOMMENDATIONS

These books and courses have been imperative to my success. I highly recommend them to you as part of your own journey.

The Secret by Rhonda Byrne. The Law of Attraction is a profound revelation that helps you get back what you put out.

The Power by Rhonda Byrne. This book shows that the power to have anything you want has been within you all the time.

Rich Dad, Poor Dad by Robert Kiyosaki. This investment bible teaches that you don't need to be born rich to have a rich mindset – you just need this book!

Frank Lowy: Pushing the Limits by Jill Margo. It's always fascinating to see how phenomenally successful people have reinvented themselves and their worlds from scratch. (Frank Lowy is one of Australia's top property developers).

Think and Grow Rich by Napoleon Hill. This self-help classic was first published during the Great Depression.

I think Hill's philosophies about harnessing desire and mastering fear in order to achieve wealth or anything you want in life hold truer than ever.

Who Moved My Cheese? by Dr Spencer Johnson. This book brilliantly illustrates the importance of adapting to unexpected change in all aspects of life.

You Don't Have To Be Born Brilliant by John McGrath. This founder of a superb real estate business believes that 'success leaves clues' and he lays out the life lessons he's learned from building wealth through real estate.

The Landmark Forum. This course, run by Landmark Education all around the world, offers so much more than self-help – course members come away completely transformed. It's an amazing opportunity to identify all the behaviours, fears, delusions and barriers that ultimately hold us all back from our own glorious potential.

Unstoppable by Cynthia Kersey 45 Powerful stories of perseverance and triumph from people just like you.

Richard Pratt: Business secrets of the billionaire behind Australia's richest private company.

Notes

_____

_____

_____

_____

_____

_____

_____

_____

_____

_____

_____

_____

_____

_____

_____

_____

_____

_____

_____

_____

_____

_____

www.LibbyLombardo.com

www.LibbyLombardo.com

CPSIA information can be obtained
at www.ICGtesting.com
Printed in the USA
BVOW08s1911110717
489093BV00016B/295/P